DEDICATION

I dedicate this book to my grandsons Kyler and Beckett Cherneski.

I wrote this book with the two of you in mind. I wanted to describe for you what society was like in the 1960s and 1970s and what society had become by 2023.

As you come to understand the issues described in this book, I hope you and your generation will be able to change the world and make it a better place.

INTRODUCTION

My name is Jerry Cherneski. I am a retired educator living in Moose Jaw, Saskatchewan. I am 74 years old and I am seriously disappointed in where our society is headed; where our political leaders, policy makers and judiciary are steering us. As I engage in discussions with people in Moose Jaw and area, a common question keeps emerging: *What's Going On?*

The way I see it, the world is wobbling out of control. Politicians make grand promises on the campaign trail, but once they are elected to office, they throw common sense out the window. And it is not just the politicians who lack sense. It is the bureaucrats who craft policy. It is even the judiciary who create legal precedent. *The Constitution Act (1982)* is being turned on its head as lawyers poke holes in what used to be common sense definitions. Dangerous laws like the *Emergency Measures Act* are being tested and talked about by our elected officials. Our country is becoming divided—thanks to social media and the AI algorithms that propagate content. As a former educator who spent his career teaching people to think and to solve problems, it seems to me there is now an up-

and-coming generation of people who cannot solve problems or critically think for themselves.

But I digress.

A few years ago, I started reflecting on life. I suppose that happens when you reach the ripe old age of 74. I suppose reflecting on life also happens when your first grandchild is born. On April 3, 2021, I was blessed with my first grandchild, Kyler. I was ecstatic, as I am sure all new grandparents are. In May 2023, I was blessed again when my second grandchild, Beckett, arrived.

Shortly after Kyler was born, I found myself codifying my reflections on life. I started making notes about how we, as Canadians, live our lives; the freedoms we once had, the freedoms we currently have, the fun things we used to do, the things we now can do, the things we cannot do, and the common sense we once enjoyed—but which has since gone missing.

I soon found myself thinking about our present democracy and comparing our current political leadership to the great politicians we have had in the past like T.C. Douglas and Jimmy Gardiner. I thought about how our government is leading our country. I asked myself whether this was the type of leadership Kyler should grow up with. I started to ruminate on the word *democracy*. I realized I had grown up in a democracy very different from today's. I started to ask myself, why is there a difference between democracy today and democracy when I was younger? Is democracy not supposed to be government by the people, of the people, for the people? I arrived at the conclusion that major laws passed by our democratically-elected government should be acceptable to at least 80% of the population.

I reflected on the concept of work. When I was growing up, almost all of us had to work; work was something we knew we had to do. I concluded that society has changed, that nowadays, not everyone wants to contribute to society. Not everyone wants to work. Many want government handouts. Others enjoy stealing from people, assaulting people; living a criminal way of life.

I found myself left with a burning question: *Where have we gone as a society?*

On December 3, 2021, Kyler was eight months old. One evening, as I sat in my favorite living room chair looking at his picture, I made a promise to him that I would work every day on this book until it was completed. Some of this novel is factual and some is fiction. Now in mid-2023, it is finally completed.

This book is dedicated to Kyler and Beckett, but dear reader, this book is also for you. As you read it, I hope you will come to agree with me that society as we used to know it has gone off the rails. I hope we can fix it before it is too late.

CHAPTER 1

I was born in 1948 on a farm near Goodeve, Saskatchewan, Canada. Goodeve, population about 250, is northwest of Melville on Highway 15. Our farm was about eight miles south of Goodeve and one mile east of the Star Blanket Reserve. Goodeve had a small grocery store. There were three implement dealers; my father liked International Harvester tractors and we had a W6 and a W9 model, as well as a Farmall model C and a Farmall model H. Goodeve had a lumber yard, and three gas stations (British American, Esso, and Royalite). The town had a locker plant, a place where you could store your frozen meat—people did not have deep freezers back then. There was also a pool hall, a curling rink, a ball diamond, and an outdoor skating rink. I recall four churches (Greek Catholic, Greek Orthodox, Roman Catholic, and Lutheran) and two schools (one for grades 1-8 and the other for grades 9-12).

I enjoyed playing hockey. One day, one of our teachers suggested we put together a team so we could play against teams from nearby towns. We ended up putting together a diverse team of 12 guys. Now that I think back on it, we did not put up with prejudice on the team—if someone made a snide remark, he would get a beating. We looked after one another. Some of the guys on the team were of German heritage, some of Ukrainian heritage, and several were from the nearby Little Black Bear First Nation. Allan Bellegarde was one of the boys from Little Black Bear. Off the ice, he was a natural, unassuming guy, but on the ice, he was tougher than nails. With Allan on our team, we seldom lost a game, and we never lost a fight. One trip playing Melville, we beat them in two back-to-back games. As the second game wrapped up, the Melville team decided they wanted to fight. It was an all-out brawl. Thanks to Allan, we won that situation. But we were never invited back to Melville again.

My family had a mixed farm. We had pigs, chickens, horses, beef cattle, dairy cows, cats, dogs and even a Shetland pony. My dad grew cereal grains: wheat, barley, and oats. In 1975, he was one of the first in our area to grow a new crop called Canola.

My two sisters, the neighbour kids, and I all took Grade 1 through Grade 8 at Robert School, eight miles away in Goodeve. I recall there being on average 20 to 22 students at the school. Sometimes we walked to school, sometimes we would hitch a cart to our horse and drive ourselves to school. Yes, in those days, we made decisions for ourselves and took responsibility to get ourselves to and from school. In the winter, we had a horse-drawn sleigh equipped with a wooden top and a little wood/coal burning stove in it to keep us warm on the journey. There was a barn at the school where we could put the horse so it would be comfortable while we were at school.

When I was five years old, my dad still had a threshing machine. We stooked sheaves of wheat in the field and then a threshing crew of men from neighbouring farms would help collect the sheaves onto wagons. Then they would feed the bundles of sheaves into the threshing machine to separate the grain from the chaff. People helped one another; farmers helped farmers and neighbours helped neighbours. In the late 1950s, Dad bought a Massey Harris number 26 combine, replacing the threshing machine and crew—and the way we harvested grain changed forever.

In 1944 with the end of the war in sight, the people of Saskatchewan elected a different kind of government; the Cooperative Commonwealth

Federation (CCF) Party. I have memories of my dad talking about the CCF Premier. He was a fine gentleman by the name of Tommy Douglas. He was a former Baptist minister who had stepped away from the pulpit to devote his life to politics and to helping the people of the province. But it was a tough go. Saskatchewan was an agricultural province. If the weather cooperated, farm families would realize a decent crop of grain. If the weather did not cooperate, crops would fail. The Douglas government tried damn hard to get the post-war economy of Saskatchewan up and running.

I can recall hearing my dad tell stories about how in the late 1940s and early 1950s, our family and some of our neighbours would sometimes need help; the Douglas government provided help through what they called "relief payments." People respected those payments because they really needed them. But people did not necessarily wait for the government to arrive with relief. In those days, neighbours would help neighbours. It was just the way things were done. The Goodeve area was quite diverse with a lot of people of Ukrainian and German descent. We all got along, enjoyed each other's company, and had respect for each other.

Life on the farm wasn't all work; we had fun too. We played sports such as hockey, baseball, fastball, and soccer. We enjoyed music; playing instruments such as the piano, guitar, accordion, banjo, and saxophone. We enjoyed visiting our neighbours, playing hockey, games like crokinole, checkers, and marbles—and of course, cards.

Growing up on the farm, we all had guns. We started out with play guns called cap guns. We would put a roll of paper caps in the guns. We would then pull the trigger and fire the caps one at a time. They would make a loud bang as they went off. I still have memories of the sulfur smell from the fired caps. Soon enough, we graduated to BB guns and then pellet guns. By the time we were around 10 years old, we graduated to using the 22-calibre rifle. The .22, as it was called, was powerful enough to shoot varmints such as gophers. The gophers would dig holes in the farm fields. A horse galloping across the field could injure his leg by stepping in a gopher hole. The .22 could also take out skunks that tried to kill our chickens. The .22 could also deal with porcupines. Farm dogs and porcupines are a bad combination. A curious dog sniffing a porcupine could easily end up with a nose and mouth full of sharp quills. There is nothing quite as distressing as using a pair of pliers to pull quills from a dog's nose. The dog would also be in anguish.

Growing up on the farm, we had a telephone. In those days, phones were not very sophisticated. We had something called the "party line." Each farmhouse on our grid road that had a telephone had their own unique ring. If the phone rang two long rings, the incoming call was for the neighbours one mile down the road. Two short rings meant the call was for the neighbour one mile in the opposite direction. At our house, we knew a call was coming in when the phone gave one long and one short ring. The problem with a party line was that when the phone rang, you could carefully pick up the receiver and listen in on your neighbour's conversations. They could do likewise and listen in on your conversations. The Saskatchewan Telephone Company asked people if they would kindly not listen to other people's calls. For people who insisted on eavesdropping, they soon earned the name "rubber-necker." Luckily, few people earned this distinctive title. Neighbours respected neighbours. Privacy was important. Now, thanks to technological leaps and bounds, we all have smart phones and have a different kind of privacy violation—frequent "robo calls" advising us that our bank account has been compromised, or our social security number has been stolen.

When we were growing up on the farm, guns were out in the open. Our dad had a rack on the back window of our half-ton truck, which would hold up to three different guns. We would drive to a nearby city or town with the guns on the rack on the window behind the seat. Not to worry, our laws and politicians said it was legal to carry guns around like this. My dad would often pass policemen on the road, his guns on full display on the window rack; the officers would give a friendly wave as the truck whizzed by. We all had guns and we learned to use them sensibly and to make sure no one ever got hurt. Common sense was the order of the day. In those days, there was not much crime. If someone, for some bizarre reason, ever wanted to break into somebody's home or building, there was a chance that a gun would be pulled out; a chance the intruder would be shot. But occurrences like this were exceedingly rare. And if a break-in ever did occur, we never heard of anyone feeling sorry for the criminal.

The neighbour boys and I eventually were old enough to get our driving licenses. We would pile into a vehicle late at night, roll the windows down and cruise the grid roads around Goodeve. We would shoot rabbits and get paid 50 cents each. This is how we made spending money. Sure, what we were doing was technically illegal, but no one cared; no one got hurt. Except for the rabbits.

One night we were driving down the road and I had to take a whiz. Maybe it was the beer we were drinking? We stopped the car, and I got out to piss. Something shiny caught my attention. It was the lights of the car reflecting off of a road sign; a sign with the speed limit posted on it. I took my 12-gauge shotgun, put a #2 cartridge in it, cocked, aimed, and pulled the trigger. The wooden post holding the sign was a 4x4 piece of lumber. Boom! The post splintered, but was still partly standing. Another shot with my shotgun and the sign came down; blown all to rat shit. The blasted sign was soon the talk among the neighbours. No one was sure who had shot the sign as we weren't the only ones that had guns. This signpost incident has never left my memory. Two shots with that 12-gauge shotgun had blown that 4x4 post in half.

A day or two later, my dad asked me if I knew anything about this sign and I confessed to him that it had been my friends and I out driving late at night, but that it was I was who had been the one shooting. I told my dad that if anyone came to our place, to do my sisters and or Mother harm, I would point the shotgun at his knees. If I knew harm would come to any of us, I would blow his leg off. My dad never said much, just looked me straight in my eyes. With a bit of a smirk on his face he said to me, "We have a few of those posts in the horse corral, let's get one and fix the sign." And fix it we did. No further questions were asked.

CHAPTER 2

Since my days of youth, the world has changed dramatically. It continues to change. And, in my opinion, not for the better. It seems like each time I read a daily paper, it has story after story about stabbings, murders, assaults, thefts, and break-ins. What is wrong with society?

The more I think about it, the more I point my finger at demographics. In the previous chapter, I described how technology came to our farm in the form of a Massey Harris combine. With that, the amount of labour needed to harvest the annual crops was reduced. No sheaves. No threshing crews of a dozen men. No threshing mills. Just my dad driving the combine through the field to harvest the grain.

Multiply this by the tens of thousands of small family farms across North America. As technology has expanded, so too has the size of farm equipment. As equipment has grown in size, so too has the size of the average farm. Over the past 40 years, we have seen a migration of people from the rural areas to the urban areas. Gone are the days of living on a farm, with the freedom of movement that open spaces provide. As society migrated towards larger population centers, individuals lost some of the independent common sense and dependence on each other that comes with rural life.

The way I figure it, the human animal is not hard-wired to live in close confines in dense population centers. As the population gravitated to larger population centers, we lost our ability to look after people. People in large population centers do not have the ability to grow their own food. People in large urban areas have to go to a job everyday; a job they potentially hate with a boss they loathe. We are not hard-wired for this density of life. People are restless.

All too often I will see a story in a newspaper about people becoming desperate, breaking into stores and stealing whatever they can. Sometimes they just walk into stores and steal what they need. Theft from retail stores is on the rise as desperate people are driven to steal what they need; what they cannot get from a caring neighbour, or from government.

A citizen doing the right thing no longer pays dividends either; a person doing the right thing by stopping a thief can have the tables turned on him quickly. Consider the case of store security guards. Security guards attempting to apprehend a thief are now sometimes vilified while the thieves are offered sympathy instead of being held responsible. As more incidents of security guards being shamed occur, fewer security guards will take action.

Consider the 2021 incident that occurred at a FreshCo grocery store in Saskatoon. According to a CBC news article, the store security guard witnessed a First Nations woman, aged 30 stealing items. He followed her out of the store, into the parking lot; an altercation ensued. He struggled her to the ground and attempted to put handcuffs on her. As he was doing this, a witness to the altercation was filming the events on a smart phone. Meanwhile, the Saskatoon Police arrived on scene. They took the woman into custody and charged her with theft under $5000 and assault. Within the hour, the Chief of the Federation of Sovereign Indigenous Nations (FSIN), weighed in with his comments. He is cited in the CBC article as saying the incident is just one more instance of the violence Indigenous women face. He said the incident was a symptom of a larger issue in the province. His exact words were: "Had that been a non-First

Nation woman, shoplifting … do you think he would have done that to that extent and assaulted her? Never." He further said if the security guard had concerns about the woman's actions, he should have taken a photo of her and recorded her licence plate number. "He took the law into his own hands, and that's wrong." The Chief said he was disturbed watching the video because he felt the woman being assaulted was in distress and if he had been there, he would have kicked the man "right in the face." He concluded, "He had no right to do that to her."

Society is spiraling out of control. Our brains are short-circuiting. A First Nations leader saying the security guard was wrong is one thing. But then for that First Nations leader to say that had he been there as the incident was unfolding, he would have assaulted the guard. Talk about taking the law into your own hands.

In the United States, the problem of urban crime is worse. Their population is ten times that of Canada so whatever rural to urban shift we have seen in Canada can be multiplied by a factor of ten. Add to this situation the waves of illegal migration that has flooded across their southern borders and we can see that large urban centers in the US are only getting larger. Add to this the effect of big box stores on the destruction of small-town America—people that used to be entrepreneurial owners of hardware stores are now working at big box stores for lousy wages. We are not hard-wired for this.

When people are desperate, and society does not look after them, they may turn to crime. Especially if that crime doesn't hold significant penalty. In 2021, according to an article in British newspaper, the *Guardian*, Walgreens closed several of its stores in San Francisco. The reason was rampant retail theft. One store video even showed a man on a bicycle riding out of a Walgreens store with a bag of stolen merchandise slung over his shoulder. In response, the City of San Francisco increased the number of officers on its retail crime unit from two to five. The City also added 13 new, unarmed community ambassadors. A non-profit organization, the *Pretrial Diversion Project*, started advocating for more mental health services like anger management classes, which it says will reduce retail theft. The Pretrial Project is also insinuating that Walgreens is racially insensitive and that local store managers have failed to make the stores a respected part of the community—this is why theft is on the rise. Theft is now not due to the thief, at least at Walgreens's stores in San Francisco. Theft is the fault of store management.

Where is this all headed? Nowhere good that's for sure.

The legal system in California takes a relatively light approach to retail theft. California Penal Code 459.5 describes the crime of shoplifting as: *entering an open business during their normal hours with intent to steal merchandise valued at $950 or less.* Under PC 459.5, shoplifting is always a misdemeanor crime and punishable by up to six months in a county jail and a fine up to $1,000, unless the defendant has one of more prior convictions. At least in theory.

According to Stanford University's social policy thinktank, the Hoover Institute, shoplifting is rampant in California because of the misdemeanor approach. Law enforcement rarely investigates a theft under this amount and if they do, prosecutors usually let them go. A 2021 article by the Hoover Institute entitled *Why Shoplifting Is Now De Facto Legal in California* explains that store employees do little to stop theft because they don't want to risk their safety when confronting a would-be thief. A confrontation within the store risks harming customers. Many retail store employees have almost certainly been instructed by their managers to do nothing. Because of this law, California is de facto extending an open invitation to anyone to walk in and take. Just like that—since thieves know that police or prosecutors won't bother with a misdemeanor complaint and that store personnel won't stop them.

Where did all this come from? The answer goes back to 2014 when California voters approved Proposition 47 which reduced the classification of most "nonserious and nonviolent property and drug crimes" from felonies to misdemeanors. An effort to repeal Proposition 47 in the 2020 state elections was voted down by 60% of voters. People complain about the increase in retail theft, yet they do nothing to change the situation when given the chance. But it gets more bizarre. Proposition 47 permits the legal system to re-sentence individuals currently serving a prison sentence for theft, reducing their charges to misdemeanors.

A 2022 article written by the Aizman Law Firm in California estimates about 10,000 inmates will be eligible for resentencing. This will certainly result in a cost savings for the California prison system. And this is where things take a bizarre twist. Proposition 47 calls for the creation of a Safe Neighbourhoods and Schools Fund. The fund will receive appropriations based on savings accrued by the state during the fiscal year, as compared to the previous fiscal year, due to the initiative's implementation. Estimates range from $150 million to $250 million per year. Reducing the severity of people's theft sentences and letting them out of jail early saves the jail system money. The State of California takes the savings and sets up a Fund to protect neighbourhoods from crime.

However, organized thieves, be aware. In September 2022, California Governor Gavin Newsom signed into law AB2294 which allows law enforcement to keep apprehended thieves in custody if they are thought to be part of an organized theft ring. Individual thieves will likely be released with a written notice or citation. Newsom also signed into law AB1700 which targets on-line sellers of merchandise thought to be stolen.

Who in hell makes these laws? To me it's insanity. Think of this, do the math: one robbery per week of $900.00 amounts to $3600 monthly. Over the course of a year, that is $43,200. If by stealing from retail stores and re-selling the goods, you could make decent money, why work? Just be sure to act alone and not in a criminal ring. This is bloody insanity!

Yes, this is an American example. If you are thinking things are different in Canada, they are not. In Canada, shoplifting (theft under $5,000) is a hybrid, criminal offence. This means that depending on the circumstances, the prosecution can decide whether the criminal charge should be a summary (misdemeanor/petty crime) or an indictable (more serious) offence. A person in Canada convicted of shoplifting charges (theft under $5,000) as a summary offence, will face a fine up to $2,000 and up to six months in prison. Then again, neither of these might apply. The courts will display leniency based on circumstances: the age of the offender, existing criminal record, whether or not threats were uttered during the crime, and so on.

I know one thing for sure. If I owned a store and was worried about being looted, I would post a sign outside my store that made it very clear to all would-be thieves. "Thieves will be greeted with blasts from my shotgun." Call me radical ….

When I think about these lax laws, I can't help but ask myself, "What is going on? Where is society headed?"

CHAPTER 3

When I was growing up in rural Saskatchewan, it was rare to hear of people with mental health issues. Nowadays, it is a different story. I believe mental illness stems from the mass migration from rural to urban that has been unfolding over the past decades. In 2018, Statistics Canada reported that an estimated 1 million Canadians live with a mental health-related disability which limits their daily life, including anxiety, depression, bipolar disorder, anorexia, and substance abuse. These are the 1 million that the health system knows about, but how many more are out there?

America is little better. An estimated 53 million Americans suffer from either PTSD, OCD, Bipolar Disorder, Social Anxiety, Schizophrenia or Clinical Depression. This is an estimated figure because this is the number that has been diagnosed. How many other people have slipped through the cracks? As society shifted into living closer together in larger centers, what happened to make so many of us mentally ill?

Science has discovered that the neurotransmitters in the brain (like serotonin, dopamine and norepinephrine) influence our moods, sleep, blood pressure, emotions, aggression levels, and even happiness. Upset the balance of these chemicals and we develop mental disease.

A 2017 study by a large team of researchers at MIT and Harvard identified the genes in our cells that are responsible for the production of these neurotransmitters are influenced by what we eat. When I was growing up in rural Saskatchewan, there was no McDonalds. There was no Burger King. A hamburger was something you made with real meat. There was no KFC. Chicken was something that Mom roasted in the oven. Nowadays, it seems we exist on processed food and fast food. Drive up and down any major street in any city and you will see a dizzying selection of fast-food joints. These places are not there to provide you with nutritional meals; their real motive is profit.

The next time you are in the grocery store, stop for a moment in any aisle. Pick a product off the shelf. Read the ingredients list. Good luck; you might need a college level chemistry book to help you. And it goes far beyond food additives. A lot of what we eat is now genetically modified. Flour, vegetables, fruits. We dine every day on GMO. The grains that farmers in Saskatchewan now grow have been genetically altered to make the plants yield more bushels to the acre. According to a Canadian government report from 1955, the 10-year trailing average for wheat yields was 17.3 bushels per acre across Alberta, Manitoba, and Saskatchewan. Nowadays, farmers on the prairies realize yields of over 40 bushels per acre on their wheat. What has changed? Science, that's what. GMO!

Research strongly suggests the additives and genetically modified organisms that are put into our food are not only causing physical health issues, but mental health issues. A 2022 Harvard University blog entitled *Nutritional psychiatry: Your brain on food* describes that the food we eat affects the kinds of bacteria that live in our guts. Upset the bacteria in the gut and we upset our chemical balances. Upset the chemical balances and the genes governing our mood and behavior come under stress. A 2015 article in *Atlantic* magazine entitled *When Gut Bacteria Change Brain Function* clearly describes how gut bacteria plays a role in generating those neurotransmitters which affect our moods.

Aside from eating, there is one other thing that we all do every day, again and again; we breathe. But what are we breathing? And how does it affect our mental health?

In 2019, the World Health Organization (WHO) estimated that worldwide 9 out of 10 people inhale polluted air. Air pollutants can affect the human brain. Affect the brain, and you affect human behavior. Gone are the days when we took ourselves to school using the family horse hooked to a wagon; breathing fresh air all the way. Today we drive cars and trucks. As we drive, we spew pollution out the tailpipe. Lots of it. Sure, our vehicles have pollution control devices—or do they?

In Germany, Volkswagen used to boast about the pollution control devices on its cars. A 2017 New York Times article describes how Volkswagen installed software on their vehicles designed to cheat the regulatory emissions tests. Some of their cars were spewing out almost 40 times the allowable amount of nitrogen oxides. What were the other automakers doing? We will likely never know. What exactly is in the air that we breathe?

Talk of exhaust emissions strikes a nerve with me. In particular, I have a strong opinion on the geopolitics of oil and natural gas. In February 2022, Vladimir Putin made an aggressive incursion into Ukraine in an effort to bring Ukraine back under the umbrella of Russian control. Controlling the Ukrainian land mass not only partly restores Russia to its former glory, it makes it very difficult for invading NATO ground forces to reach Moscow undeterred.

What many people do not give thought to is the fact that Russia is a major energy player and has used its energy reserves to anticipate military aggression against Ukraine. Russia is the second largest oil producer among the OPEC+ nations, flowing 9.7 million barrels a day. Russia is also a huge natural gas player with an estimated 6,923 trillion cubic feet of natural gas reserves. (Canada by comparison has an estimated 1,373 trillion cubic feet.) Russia supplies many European nations with oil and gas. In 2008, Angela Merkel of Germany and Nicolas Sarkozy of France blocked Ukraine's appeal to join NATO. Think about it. They were afraid. Russia had politicized its energy supply. Mr. Putin made it

What's Going On?

clear—your country wants energy from Russia? Then you better do what Russia demands of you, even if that means denying Ukraine admittance into NATO. But sometimes even the best-envisioned strategies fail. In late 2022, somebody (we will never know who) detonated underwater charges and blew up the two Nord Stream pipelines carrying natural gas from Russia to Germany. The pipelines are now ruined. Repairing them will require assistance from western nations along with tens of billions of dollars. All that natural gas in Russia is now stranded. The economic blow to Russia is staggering. But the EU is also staggering. Absent the Nord Stream supply, the EU will now be forced to import its natural gas from either the US or from Qatar in liquefied (LNG) format. In either case, the cost of obtaining natural gas to power manufacturing in Germany and surrounding countries has now tripled.

As I finish this manuscript, the situation in the Ukraine has been going on now for over 12 months. There is no end in sight. The casualties continue to mount. NATO, and the USA in particular, is supplying armaments to Ukraine. And not just guns and bullets; very sophisticated, hi-tech weaponry. The inventory list provided by the State Department is staggering. The price tag for this contribution is now over $13 billion and this conflict looks set to drag on for a very long time.

In 2010, Canadian company TC Energy began plans to lay a 36-inch diameter pipeline (the Keystone XL pipeline) to move 830,000 barrels a day of heavy crude oil from Alberta to refineries in the mid-West and along the Gulf coast. With the route planned out, and with the pipe being made, all that remained was to start construction. But, a change of government in the USA caused a roadblock. In November of 2015, the Obama administration vetoed the pipeline. Obama caved to the threats of environmentalists who said that the pipeline posed a danger to climate, ecosystems, drinking water and basic public health. Donald Trump brought the project back to life with a fight against all the legal battles against it. He argued the project would support 42,000 jobs over its two-year construction period and hundreds of permanent jobs thereafter. January 21, 2021, was the first day in office for Joe Biden. One of the first things he did was to kill the Keystone XL pipeline. Environmental activists were thrilled about the cancellation.

Here is where the lack of common sense is on full display. What people fail to understand is that there is no *one thing* called Oil. Oil from different geographic regions have different densities. Oil density is measured in API units. Oil from Texas is around API 40. Oil from North Dakota is around API 43. All the shale oil currently being produced in the US is around API 58. A typical oil and gas refinery in the US is designed to accept API 40 oil into the process. All that API 58 shale oil being produced in the US has to be blended with heavier oil (around API 22). This is the only way that the shale oil can be made suitable to feed into the refineries. And where does the heavy API 22 oil come from? Well, hello! It comes from western Canada. But the politicians could not figure that out. Instead, they cancelled the Keystone XL project.

But here is where it gets twisted. Joe Biden's decision to kill the Keystone XL project made Warren Buffet very happy. Mr. Buffet, through his Berkshire Hathaway fund, owns BNSF Railway and its fleet of tanker railcars that can transport oil. President Biden's decision to kill the Keystone XL project no doubt made Justin Trudeau very happy also, although he has carefully concealed his feelings on the matter. The way I see it, Mr. Trudeau has been against the oil and gas industry since coming to office. This political slant has emboldened Canadian environmentalists who in turn express their gratitude at the ballot box. I figure old Pierre Trudeau schooled young Justin well. I can envision young Justin sitting on his father's knee listening to stories of how Daddy created the National Energy Plan to redistribute oil wealth from western Canada back to eastern Canada.

Speaking of environmentalists, let's take a closer look at what this is all about. About 6,000 products are made or are partially made from oil and gas. To name a few: plastics, lubricants, waxes, tars, asphalt for our roads, nylon fabric, acrylics, rayon, fake leather, polyester, spandex, diapers, dishwashing liquid, solar panels, food preservatives, DVDs, electronic speakers, smartphones, computers, cameras, televisions, and even tires on our vehicles. The manufacturing of all forms of transportation including airplanes, motorcycles, bicycles, trains, cars, boats, scooters, skateboards, and even electric vehicles requires petroleum-based plastic products. Unless they are made of leather, your shoes are likely made of petrochemicals which impart lightweight, durability and water-resistant properties. Are you a sporting fan? Most common sports equipment such as basketballs, golf balls and golf bags, football helmets, surfboards, skies, tennis rackets, fishing rods, hockey skates (the boot part) and hockey pucks contain some form of petroleum. (As a kid on the farm, we used frozen cow pies as hockey pucks. If there were no cow pies, frozen horse droppings worked just fine too. No fossil fuels used in those pucks.)

Years ago, when I was a kid, toys were made from metal. When metal toys were deemed to be dangerous, toys started being made from plastics. Our health care industry relies heavily on petroleum products: pacemakers, MRI machines, IV bags and tubes, surgical instruments, monitors and stethoscopes, heart valves, eyeglasses, contact lenses, prosthetics, hearing aids, dentures, soaps, and antiseptics, and aspirin. Yes, that's right. Aspirin. The starting product for the chemical synthesis of aspirin is benzene, a petroleum product. Benzene is then converted to phenol which in turn is converted to salicylic acid which is then converted to acetylsalicylic acid, the stuff we call aspirin. Petroleum products are also synthesized into the many life saving pharmaceuticals used by emergency care doctors and physicians.

Let's look at the homes where we live: construction materials such as roofing, housing, insulation, linoleum flooring, caulking, furniture, appliances, pillows, curtains, rugs, house paint, and many other everyday kitchen items including dishes, cups, non-stick pans and many dish detergents use oil in their creation. Just a few other things I will mention: motor oil, bearing grease, insecticides, ballpoint pens, nail polish, perfumes, clothing, transparent tape, faucet washers, deodorants, refrigerant (let's get rid of things that need refrigeration and the oil to lubricate the compressors), battery cases, fertilizers, most toilet seats (those could be replaced with wooden ones), water pipes and parachutes. Try to imagine living without these products!

Suppose a person is against guns; they call themselves anti-gun lobbyists. They do not own a gun, shells, or anything related to guns or firearms. Fair enough, so be it. But what about the anti-pipeline, anti-oil environmentalist? If they are true to their conviction, then they should not use any of the products that I have just listed. How would they live? I guess somewhere in a log house, with a wood burning stove or furnace. They would have wooden floors, wooden furniture, pure cotton blankets. They would have no computer, no internet, and no cell phone. How would they get around? Car, no. Even an electric car has oil-based components like tires and plastic body parts. Even if they chose to overlook that detail, they could not drive on pavement because it is made with oil-based products. How about a bicycle? No, because of the synthetic rubber tires. They would have to walk on gravel roads with leather shoes, or leather moccasins. The other option would be to go barefoot.

Do these so-called environmentalists have children? Where were their kids born? Surely not in a hospital with all its petroleum-based products. They could not have used a midwife; she would have probably had a gas-burning car, manufactured using petroleum-based products. Do these environmentalists eat? What about the rubber-tired delivery transport trucks that traveled across asphalt roads to deliver produce to their local grocery stores?

How are environmentalists educating their kids? Surely not in a school containing horrible oil and gas related products such as plastic furniture, painted walls, and computers? Maybe they are home schooling their young ones with laptops, smart phones, internet, and more petroleum-based things. I have to laugh. I keep hearing how environmentalists want no part of oil and gas, yet without it none of them could live.

Earlier, I wrote that when I was growing up, we would often visit the neighbours. We would get together with the neighbour kids to play board games and card games. That was our way of socializing. Games were our social media. Nowadays, its different. We socialize using hand-held smart phones and tablets. We have laptop computers. We are all connected to the Internet.

This brings me back to the idea that as we all crowd into larger urban centers we are becoming unsettled, disturbed. Practically living on smart phones and tablets is only making the situation worse.

The circumstance of Ryan Grantham in BC is a case in point. In early 2020, when Grantham was 21 years old, he shot his mother in the back of her head with a .22 rifle as she played piano in their Squamish townhouse. A GoPro video Grantham took a short time after the murder was presented as evidence in court. In the video, he confesses to the murder and shows his mother's body. The next day, he covered the body with a sheet, arranged lit candles around it and hung a rosary from the piano before driving off in a car packed with guns, ammunition and Molotov cocktails, with the intention of travelling east to Ottawa to kill Prime Minister Justin Trudeau. He drove to Hope, BC, where he turned around with new thoughts of committing a mass shooting at Simon Fraser University where he was enrolled, or possibly a mass shooting on the Lions Gate Bridge. Later that night, he drove to the Vancouver Police Department building in East Vancouver and turned himself in.

In her comments, the judge called it a "saving grace" that Grantham had enough attachment to reality and psychological comprehension to elect not to go on a shooting rampage. She summarized how Grantham was in a downward spiral in the months leading up to the matricide, spending an increasing amount of time smoking cannabis and watching violent videos on the dark web, while feeling isolated and consumed by suicidal and homicidal urges. The judge said she considered Grantham's mental health difficulties at the time of the murder a mitigating circumstance. She sentenced him to life in prison, but he will be eligible for parole in 14 years.

Violent videos. The dark web. Feeling isolated. Having suicidal and homicidal urges. The judge in the Grantham case nailed it square on as far as I am concerned. All this connectedness is affecting our brains. We are shorting out. We are slowly spiraling downwards. In 2020, the documentary film *Social Dilemma* was nominated for seven Emmy Awards. This powerful film looked at the ugly reality of the big social media outlets. Tech giants like Facebook and Google have created AI algorithms to create a false sense of urgency and distraction. How many texts do you get each day? How many emails pop up on your smart phone? How many things pop up on your Facebook page? Go to YouTube. Watch a video. The next time you visit YouTube, you will be inundated with video ideas of a similar genre. This is the AI algorithms at work. When our phones bing or ding, our brain is alerted that something is urgent. We lose our ability to focus on the task we are doing; there is something urgent to tend to. The next time you are in a group setting, sit back and watch people. Notice where their focus lies. It isn't on the other people in the group—it is on their phones. They need the stimulation from notifications binging and dinging. They need the stimulation from reading Facebook posts. How many hours per day do you spend on your phone or tablet?

Thanks to Mark Zuckerberg and his team at Meta, this situation is only going to get darker. Our hand-held devices might soon allow us to run; to escape. Very soon we will be able to put a set of goggles on and tap into the metaverse. Want to fight terrorists in a war zone? Slap on the metaverse goggles and enter a parallel universe. Video game maker Roblox is already hard at work designing the dark games that we will soon have available in the metaverse. But it is not a group of people at Roblox who are creating the games. The code for the games is being written by gamers living in their moms' basements. Roblox will pay these at-home programmers a royalty on games they create.

Do you remember a political giant from the 1970s by the name of Henry Kissinger? He turned 100 years of age in May 2023. In 2021, he authored a book along with Google pioneer Eric Schmidt and MIT professor Daniel Huttenlocher. The book is titled *Age of AI*. The opening lines of chapter six are powerful: *In an age in which machines increasingly perform tasks only humans used to be capable of, what will constitute our identity as human beings? AI will expand what we know of reality. It will alter how we communicate, network, and share information. When we no longer explore and shape reality on our own—when we enlist AI as an adjunct—how will we come to see ourselves and our role in the world?*

I do not like where all this technology is taking us. What do you think?

What's Going On?

In her book, *Dopamine Nation*, author Dr. Anne Lembke does not mince words on the subject. She writes: "The smartphone is the modern-day hypodermic needle, delivering digital dopamine 24/7 for a wired generation. As such, we've all become vulnerable to compulsive overconsumption." She would know. She is the Medical Director of Addiction Medicine at Stanford and has spent 25-plus years treating patients with all sorts of addictions.

At the start of this book, I made it very clear that growing up on the farm, I was happy. We were all happy. We had each other. We had our friends at school. We had our parents. Nowadays, not everyone is so lucky. Some children grow up surrounded by parents and siblings who are messed up. They eat poorly, they are exposed to toxins. Children end up being bullied, abused, and discriminated against. They develop mental health issues just like their parents and siblings. A 2010 study at Harvard University, entitled *The Foundations of Lifelong Health Are Built in Early Childhood*, needs no further explanation.

Too many people spend their lives running away from the bad memories of growing up. A traumatic event can bring a flood of memories back. Memories that were once buried now sear painfully through the brain. This is called PTSD (post traumatic stress disorder). Mental health professionals used to think that PTSD was only something that soldiers and first responders had to worry about. It turns out, nearly eight million adults in the United States struggle with this condition every single year. That's 3.6% of the population. Data from Statistics Canada reports that 10% of Canadian women and 6% of men have PTSD and that a staggering percentage (13%) of young adults have PTSD. Traumatic events from the past affect how we interact with the world.

If you think that all this scientific banter about mental illness is just the stuff of academic articles, I assure you it is not. People shy away from talking about an incident that occurred in 2008 on a Greyhound Bus travelling between Saskatchewan and Manitoba along the Trans Canada highway. This 2008 incident highlights the whole mental health issue.

It was July 30, 2008. Bus number 1170 from Edmonton to Winnipeg was right on schedule. One of the passengers on board was 22-yearold

Tim McLean. Mr. McLean was on his way home to Winnipeg; he had been working for the carnival midway in Edmonton. Witnesses who were on the bus say that McLean sat at the back of the bus in a window seat, with his headphones on, minding his own business.

Twenty-four hours earlier on July 29, 2008 a similar story had played out on a Greyhound Bus going from Edmonton to Winnipeg. One of the passengers getting on board was 40-year-old Vince Li. He and his wife had emigrated from China to Canada in 2001 and he was granted Canadian citizenship in 2006. He had difficulty finding work despite having a degree in computer science from Wuhan University and at one point had worked as a church custodian in Winnipeg and had spent time in a mental health institution in Ontario. In 2006, he left his wife and moved to Edmonton where he found work delivering newspapers, then serving at McDonalds, and finally clerking at Walmart. After a falling out with a supervisor at Walmart in 2008, Li decided to head back to Winnipeg. He packed his bags and boarded the Greyhound bus for the 18-hour trip.

At a scheduled stop in Erickson, Manitoba, Li got off the bus with three pieces of luggage. He did not get back on the bus. A witness interviewed by police said he saw Li sitting on a park bench in Erickson at 3 a.m. in the morning; bags of luggage beside him. The next morning, July 30, a young lad from Erickson was riding his bike through town when he spotted Mr. Li still on the park bench. This time, Mr. Li had a laptop computer open with a for sale sign on it. The young lad paid Li $60 for the laptop.

Mr. Li remained in Erickson for the remainder of the day. Around 6 p.m., the Greyhound bus rolled into town and made its scheduled stop. Mr. Li had purchased a ticket from Erickson to Winnipeg. He boarded the bus and took a seat near the front. Before long, the bus resumed its journey. The next stop would be Brandon, Manitoba. Witnesses state that at Brandon, Li got off the bus and smoked a cigarette, not speaking to anyone else. When he re-boarded the bus, he made his way to the back of the bus and sat right beside Tim McLean. Soon enough the bus pulled out and began heading for its next stop, Portage la Prairie, Manitoba located about 30 km from Winnipeg. But the bus would not make it to Portage la Prairie. Something tragic was about to happen.

As the bus rolled long the Trans Canada highway, heading for Portage la Prairie, suddenly, in one swift move, Vince Li pulled out a knife and stabbed Tim McLean.

Passengers began screaming; the bus driver pulled over to the side of the road and brought the bus to a screeching halt. All the passengers could do was run from the bus onto the highway. Someone with a cell phone called the police (RCMP); it took several minutes for the police to arrive. Meanwhile, Li kept stabbing McLean. As the RCMP arrived on scene, Vince Li was eating the head of Tim McLean; cannibalizing him.

Had someone had a gun … well, I think you get my point. Call me radical.

The police never having seen such a gory mess, gently arrested Vince Li and removed him from the bus. Li was charged with second degree murder. Li told investigators that he heard what he believed was *The Voice of God*. "The voice told me that I was the third story of the Bible, that I was like the second coming of Jesus and that I was to save people from a space alien attack."

On March 5, 2009, 40-year-old Vince Li was found not criminally responsible and was remanded to a high security mental health facility in Selkirk, Manitoba. As time went on, the media offered up what they knew about Vince Li, which was not much. By June of 2010, Li had been granted supervised outdoor walks within the mental health facility. By May 30, 2011, his psychiatric doctor was arguing for more freedoms. On May 17, 2012, Li was granted temporary passes that allowed him out of the Selkirk, Manitoba health centre. He could visit the town of Selkirk (population of about 11,000), supervised by a nurse or police officer. In 2012, Li was interviewed by the Schizophrenia Society of Canada. The Society's CEO said that there was under a 7% chance that Li would re-offend. By 2013, he was allowed more supervised visits to nearby beaches.

By February 2015, Li had been given unsupervised day passes to visit Winnipeg with the proviso that he carried a functioning cellular phone. In early February 2016, he changed his name to Will Baker and applied to leave his group home and live independently. In February 26, 2016, he was granted the right to live alone; courtesy of the Criminal Code Review Board.

I have seen many things in my 74 years. This Vince Li thing is truly unbelievable. The Criminal Code Review Board is an arm of the federal government. The message was loud and clear. If you are insane, you can board a public vehicle, cut someone's head off, cannibalize that person, cause stress to all people on that bus, cause the suicide of an investigating police officer (in July 2014, one of the first officers on the scene—RCMP Corporal Ken Barker—committed suicide), and then be granted the right to live on your own, all within eight years of committing the crime.

Hold it—we are not done! One of the passengers on the bus at the time of the incident suffered from mental illness. Several years later, she gave birth to a child. And get this: social workers had her newborn apprehended because they were concerned that the post-traumatic stress disorder (PTSD) stemming from the attack made her unfit to care for her newborn daughter. The baby spent the first 18 months of her life in a foster home before being returned to the mother. Can you believe it? And it gets even worse. A truck driver passing by saw the bus pulled over and people in a panic. He stopped his truck and ran to assist. He helped barricade the bus door shut so Li could not escape. As he glanced up, he could see Li through a window holding Timothy McLean's head and cannibalizing it. To this day, this truck driver has to consume alcohol every night to help him get to sleep and get the memories out of his head. On February 10, 2017, not quite 10 years after this sick tragedy happened, the Manitoba Criminal Code Review Board granted Vince Li an absolute discharge with no legal obligations, no restrictions, no monitoring, no reporting. The Board said, "He did not pose a significant threat." Vince Li/Will Baker was free to go. This is not fiction. This really happened. Vince Li/Will Baker is free under Canadian laws.

Government by the people, of the people, for the people? Really? Is this why my grandfather emigrated from Europe? Is this why my grandfather and my father developed calluses on their hands as they worked the farm to build a better life? Is this the type of leadership my grandson Kyler has to look forward to?

When I was growing up, had someone pulled a knife as Vince Li did, we would have taken matters into our own hands. He would have had one hell of a severe beating laid on him. That is how things were done in those days.

But not these days. People today are afraid to help others. We are not hard-wired to live in crowded urban centers. We are losing our common sense. A security guard in Saskatoon is vilified for trying to apprehend a shoplifter. The food we eat is messed up. The air we breath is messed up. The toxins we take into our bodies are ruining our mental health. The social media platforms we live on for hours each day are robbing us of our social skills. We are anxious. We are mentally sick.

What have our governments done? Nothing, to be blunt. Nothing, other than pass law after law after law to regulate our behavior. When I was growing up, we did not have all these laws. We had the law of common sense. Today, we have a distinct lack of common sense. Government has turned Canadian citizens into cowards! Is this the way we should live? I certainly hope my grandsons never have to live this way.

What do you think about it all—mental illness, pollution, social media and AI, geopolitics? What is going on?

CHAPTER 4

As society slowly spirals down and short circuits, we are dividing into what seems like two camps: those of means and privilege and those without. In my opinion, our elected officials have made (and are making) laws that ordinary citizens have to follow but citizens of means and privilege do not. Consider the Hockey Canada debacle.

On June 18, 2018, Hockey Canada held a gala and golf event in London, Ontario. Founded in 1914, Hockey Canada is the national governing body of the sport. It is responsible for growing and administering the game at grassroots levels, as well as managing national teams and bidding to host International Ice Hockey Federation events like the World Juniors and World Hockey Championship.

In attendance at the gala were members of the Canadian men's junior hockey team; all under the age of twenty. The next day, a man called the Hockey Canada Vice President of Human Resources to say that his step-daughter had been sexually assaulted in her hotel room by a group of players. This complaint was relayed to CEO Tom Renney who in turn contacted the London, Ontario police. Renney then contacted the Board members to apprise them of what was happening. Hockey Canada retained the services of law firm Henein Hutchison LLP. The players alleged to have been involved were then contacted. They were told they could participate in any investigations if they wanted to; choice was theirs. The players' NHL teams were then apprised and told they could become involved if they so chose. Henein Hutchinson then compiled a report for Hockey Canada advising on courses of action that would be taken.

CEO Tom Renney had been brought aboard by Hockey Canada in 2014 following his career as a coach in the National Hockey League, which included head-coaching stints with the Vancouver Canucks, New York Rangers, and Edmonton Oilers. During his two years behind the bench for the Vancouver Canucks (1996-1998), he was paid a total of US $477,000. As he announced his retirement with tears in his eyes, he spoke glowingly of his replacement Tom Smith.

In April 2022, the young woman in question (who can only be identified as E.M.) filed a statement of claim ($3.5 million) in the Courts against Hockey Canada. Her statement of claim said the hockey players brought golf clubs to the hotel room to further intimidate her, directed her to shower after the sexual assault, and told her to say she was sober while they videotaped a consent video.

When news of the statement of claim became public, the politicians got involved and started to probe the matter. On June 2, 2022, members of Hockey Canada's executive appeared before a House of Commons committee where questions were asked about the sexual assault incident. CEO Tom Renney told the committee, "Our message to anyone who feels they are a victim of maltreatment by someone affiliated with Hockey Canada is that we want to hear from you. We are committed to ensuring that we are a safe space for raising your concerns." Renney offered the following explanation to the House of Commons standing committee, "With regard to the legal action that was filed in April of this year, we settled the claim quickly because we felt a moral obligation to respond to the alleged behaviour that occurred at one of our events by players who attended at our invitation. While we don't know exactly what occurred that night or the identities of those involved, we recognize that the conduct was unacceptable and incompatible with Hockey Canada's values and expectations, and that it clearly caused harm. We felt that the right response to the woman's legal request was one that did not require her to participate in a prolonged court proceeding. The settlement enables her to seek whatever support she might require as she tries to move past this incident."

Grilled by a Liberal member of the committee, Renney said, "We took the responsibility on the basis that we wanted to respect the young woman's right to privacy. You can appreciate that we've known about this since June 2018. We received the statement of claim through the Canadian Hockey League. We took responsibility to speak to the plaintiff's counsel, and we entered into settlement discussions immediately."

Several heavy-weight sponsors including Bauer, Tim Hortons, Canadian Tire, Scotiabank, and Esso have since dropped their financial support of Hockey Canada. In late October 2022, Hockey Canada announced that a third-party investigator had completed its examination of the incident. The report will remain confidential. An independent adjudication panel will determine what, if any, sanctions will be imposed on anyone involved in the incident. Meanwhile, the London Police Service has re-opened its investigation into the entire matter.

The case has now been settled out of court; the names of the players have not been released. When the London Police Service investigated the matter, it was discovered this was not the first such case for Hockey Canada. The organization even had a special fund, made up from registration fee revenues, to deal with sexual assault claims.

In the aftermath of the Commons committee investigation, the entire management team from Hockey Canada resigned.

As Hockey Canada management members were resigning, board member Andrea Skinner stepped up to act as Hockey Canada's interim chair. She brazenly argued that the problems Hockey Canada faced with sexual misconduct were reflective of a broader societal problem. She was then pressured into resigning.

What's Going On?

Talk about utter bullshit. Players from the assault event not required to cooperate with investigators? Can you believe this? A fund to cover up sexual assault claims? Confidential reports? Is this what Canada's national sport has degraded into? What about all the kids out there who want to play hockey? How has the hockey business degraded to this low? Let's hope the public shaming of Hockey Canada will now see some honest people get involved.

A set of laws for those of means and privilege goes way beyond Hockey Canada. I am downright pissed about how some members of society can hide money offshore and sidestep the Canada Revenue Agency. For little guys like me, I would not have a clue how to go about hiding money. But if you are a person of means and influence, it seems that it is rather easy to hide money.

Take the case of the *Panama Papers*. I have never been to Panama. But I know a guy from Mossbank, Saskatchewan who went to Panama in 2019. He told me when his flight was coming into the Panama City airport, he looked out his window. For a moment, he thought he was coming into Miami or Los Angeles. The entire waterfront was nothing but gleaming high-rise buildings. He told me one night he was out for a walk around his hotel. He noticed something very odd. In all of these tall buildings, there was scarcely a light on. The next morning, he started a conversation with a local woman who was walking her dog. He asked her about the tall buildings with no lights on. He asked her who lived in those tall buildings. She looked at him as if he was a bit daft. She shook her head and explained, "Nobody lives in them. The units are owned by people from offshore. That's one of the ways they move money out of their countries. They buy a bunch of condominiums in Panama City and leave them vacant. When they need some cash, they find a real estate agent who has a network of unsuspecting people from the US or Canada all seeking to buy a dream property in Panama. Money changes hands through a law office in Panama and with that, money has been laundered."

In early 2016, the proverbial shit finally hit the fan. Somebody in Panama leaked a massive database of names and account details to the *International Consortium of Investigative Journalists* (ICIJ). In all, 11.5

million confidential documents were leaked; all stemmed back to the Panama-based law office of Mossack Fonseca. This was not just any law office, It was the fourth-biggest offshore law firm in the world. A German newspaper, *Süddeutsche Zeitung*, decided to run with the story. The name "Panama Papers" was given to the leaked documents. The damage from the fallout was staggering. It revealed a web of opaque shell companies, shadowy lawyers, and complicit banks. In all, a total of 214,488 offshore entities (individuals and shell companies) were listed. By November 2016, Europol reported that it had found 3,469 probable matches to criminal and terrorist organizations when they compared the Panama Papers to their own files. The Prime Ministers of Iceland and Pakistan were forced to resign. Canada's Royal Bank closed more than 40 bank accounts immediately after the Panama Papers were made public.

In October 2017, another swathe of data was provided to the German newspaper, *Süddeutsche Zeitung*. This data came from the offshore law firm Appleby. This leaked data has been given the name the *Paradise Papers*.

In October 2021, the plot thickened further with the release of the *Pandora Papers*. Same scenario. A British Virgin Islands organization called Trident Trust leaked 3.3 million data records to the International Consortium of Investigative Journalists (ICIJ); the same consortium that had been given the Mossack Fonseca (Panama Papers) data in 2016. The Pandora leak has exposed the secret offshore accounts of 35 world leaders, including current and former presidents, prime ministers, and heads of state as well as more than 100 billionaires, celebrities, and business leaders. The ICIJ is still sifting through the data but they figure up to $32 trillion in hidden money could be at stake.

In Canada, nearly 900 individuals and companies have been identified from the leaked documents. The Canada Revenue Agency has identified more than $76 million in taxes owed by Canadians named in the Panama Papers. And that list of Canadians includes, well … we will see. No charges have been laid. No criminal investigations have been launched. The Revenue Agency people are not talking. NDP finance critic and Manitoba MP Niki Ashton says, "The answers from the CRA are shocking." She added, "It really speaks to the way in which the Canadian government ... is not going after the ultra-rich who are getting away with tax evasion and avoiding their taxes."

Data reveals that from 2004 to 2009, former prime Minister Brian Mulroney was a director of Said Holdings Limited, a Bermuda company controlled by controversial Syrian-Saudi businessman Wafic Said. The company, created in 1994, had other directors, including Lord Powell of Bayswater, a former top foreign policy adviser to Margaret Thatcher, and Robert Zoellick, former president of the World Bank. Did Mulroney do anything wrong with respect to tax evasion or avoidance? We many never know. The shell companies that were created by these offshore law firms are like a spider web.

Some of the data reveals that Stephen Bronfman, Justin Trudeau's adviser and close friend, teamed up with Liberal Party strategist Leo Kolber to quietly move millions of dollars to a Cayman trust.

More data shows that Bermuda-registered Madagascar Oil Limited awarded stock options to Prime Minister Chretien in July 2007 as a consulting fee. Chretien has admitted he did a few days work for Madagascar Oil but he denies ever having been granted stock options.

Retired figure skater Elvis Stojko had a life insurance policy on his parents. The policy was set up so that upon their demise the $6.5 million payout would go to a special fund run by Skate Canada for athletes to use to legally shelter income and protect their amateur status. Stojko does not know how, but his Montreal lawyer changed the life insurance policy to instead pay out to a trust in Belize called the Quad Trust.

In 2010, former race car driver Jacques Villeneuve declared $6,431 in personal income and also claimed a tax credit for low-income families. The next two years, he declared $3,224 and $5,782 in income. Meanwhile, his career winnings and corporate endorsement fees were sitting a British Virgin Islands trust fund. The fund then invested in a Bahamas company called Goldstar Holdings; without any paper trail. Long story short, Mr. Villeneuve is living a tax-free lifestyle.

I look forward to the financial sleuths at ICIJ revealing more names of Canadians who are tangled up in the offshore tax avoidance game. Everyone should pay their fair share of taxes. No exceptions. No excuses.

But somehow, I doubt much progress will be made on the offshore tax game. As I was writing this manuscript, I read the summary of a 2016 report entitled *The Canada Revenue Agency, Tax Avoidance and Tax Evasion: Recommended Actions*. This report prepared by the House of Commons Standing Committee on Finance called upon a number of tax experts. One organization, the *Quebec Tax Justice Network*, pulled no punches. It told the hearing the federal government is not very committed to addressing the issue of tax havens and that world leaders from a number of countries responded to the "Panama Papers" in a more forceful manner than did Canada's Prime Minister. The organization *Canadians for Tax Fairness* told the committee that Canada's federal and provincial governments stand to lose between $5.3 billion and $7.3 billion annually as a result of tax avoidance and evasion.

And then, I stumbled on a bombshell; a rather perverted bombshell at that. It turns out that while the House of Commons committee was putting on its 2016 investigative show of how to deal with tax evasion and avoidance, offshore law firms were recommending to their clients to use Canada to dodge tax. It turns out that under Canadian corporate law, a person from offshore can set up a Limited Partnership (a L.P.). That L.P. is not required to pay taxes or undergo audits.

I give up. Far too many people of means and privilege are showing a disconnect to the rest of civil society. It is my hope that my grandsons go on to be a financially successful. But I do hope they never behave as though they are privileged and better than everyone else.

Prime Minister Trudeau comes from a privileged background. The family money was made by his grandfather, Charles-Emile Trudeau. Charles-Emile was a lawyer, but he developed a network of 30 gas stations in the Montreal area. He eventually sold this venture for $1 million to a larger corporation. This is the money that allowed his son Pierre to be educated at the Sorbonne in Paris. This is the money that funded Pierre's meteoric rise in politics; from MP in 1965 to Prime Minster in 1968.

What's Going On?

Wealth begets wealth. A good chunk of the family wealth found its way to son Justin Trudeau.

Prime Minister Justin Trudeau has, on occasion, displayed a disconnect to the average person on the street. In December 2016, Trudeau took his family on a trip to a private island in the Bahamas owned by the Aga Khan; actually, His Highness Prince Karim Aga Khan IV. The Aga Khan was born Karim al-Husayn Shah in Geneva, Switzerland, on December 13, 1936. He grew up in Nairobi, studied in Switzerland and then graduated from Harvard University. He is the 49th hereditary Imam (spiritual leader) of the world's 15 million Shia Ismaili Muslims. The title "His Highness" was formally granted to him by Queen Elizabeth II upon the death of his grandfather, Aga Khan III.

The Muslim faith traces its origins to the Prophet Muhammed. The Muslim faith became divided when Muhammed died. Some of Muhammed's followers believed that Muhammed did not make provision for a successor. These followers went on to form the Sunni sect of the Muslim faith. The Shia sect believed that Muhammed had appointed his son-in-law to lead the faithful. The Ismaili Muslims are a subset of the Shia sect and believe their leaders are the descendants of the sixth Shia Imam, His Highness Prince Karim Aga Khan IV is one of those descendants.

As spiritual leader, the Aga Khan's responsibilities include interpreting the faith and looking after the spiritual and material well-being of his followers, which means helping improve the quality of life of the community in the societies where they live. The Aga Khan is founder and chairman of a major international aid organization—the Aga Khan Development Network (AKDN). The AKDN is a vast network of agencies that employs 80,000 people in 30 countries and is best known for the work it does in some of the poorest parts of the globe. Since 2004, the Canadian government has sponsored 16 global development initiatives in partnership with the foundation, worth a total of more than $300 million. The various projects have included supporting craft producers in Mozambique to investing in childhood education in Bangladesh to working to improve women's health in Afghanistan.

Through it all, the Aga Khan has become very wealthy with a net worth pegged at $800 million. How did he amass this fortune? It turns out that Ismaili Muslims Ismailis are obliged to tithe, giving 10% of their earnings to the Aga Khan, which he in turn invests in the charity network. As for the connection between Canada and the Agha Khan, the relationship with the Trudeaus goes back to the 1970s when Ugandan dictator Idi Amin expelled Ismailis from his country. The Aga Khan called on then-Prime Minister Pierre Trudeau to give his people a safe haven, and Canada took in 7,000 Ismailis.

Did Trudeau do the right thing by visiting the Agha Khan at his private island? In December 2017, Mary Dawson, federal ethics commissioner, found Trudeau had contravened four sections of the *Federal Conflict of Interest Act*. She said the holiday could be seen as a gift designed to influence the Prime Minister. She noted in her report that the Aga Khan Foundation is a registered lobby in Canada and that it had received over $50 million of federal funding in 2016 alone.

While other Prime Ministers and politicians have met the Agha Khan in Ottawa, Justin Trudeau decided to go to the Aga Khan's private island. That decision by Justin Trudeau made it very clear to Canadians that there is one set of rules for himself and one set for everyone else. The question I ask is: Why did not Trudeau's inner circle of advisors warn him about the potential conflict of interest and the poor optics of it all? As far as I am concerned, this is an absolute disgrace to democracy! And that's putting it rather mildly.

Another scandal Justin Trudeau was involved in was the SNC-Lavalin case. SNC Lavalin is a global engineering company headquartered in Quebec. SNC had been found guilty of paying bribes in developing nations in efforts to secure engineering contracts. Trudeau tried to pressure his Justice Minister, Jody Wilson-Raybould, to drop criminal corruption charges against the company and instead issue financial penalties. Had SNC been charged and found guilty, it would not been able to bid on federal contracts for ten years. As Trudeau and Wilson-Raybould scrapped and argued with each other, on March 29, 2019, she secretly recorded a telephone call between herself and Privy Council Clerk Michael Wernick.

The audio tape clearly has Wernick telling Wilson-Raybould that Trudeau wanted a deferred prosecution agreement for SNC-Lavalin "one way or another." On April 2, 2019, when Trudeau found out about the tape, he expelled Wilson-Raybould from the Liberal caucus in the House of Commons and stripped her of the Liberal Party nomination for the 2019 Canadian federal election. Trudeau said her secretly recording her conversation with the Privy Council Clerk was "unconscionable." The ethics commissioner found Trudeau guilty of violating ethics rules. But he is still the Prime Minister. One set of rules for him, one set for the rest of us.

Trudeau's disregard for ethics was again on full display with the WE Charity scandal. In 2020, the WE Charity was awarded a federal government contract to administer the $912 million Canada Student Summer Grant program. The shit hit the fan when it was revealed that the WE charity had previously paid Trudeau's mother and brother to appear at its events. It was soon revealed that the WE Charity paid approximately $425,000 to Trudeau's family. What's more, the WE Charity also used pictures of Trudeau's family members as celebrity endorsements in their marketing efforts. Trudeau defended himself by arguing that the WE Charity was "the only possible option," for administering the program. He further claimed it was the civil service, not he, who decided that WE Charity was the best option. Finance Minister Bill Morneau ducked out the back door and exited politics when it was revealed his daughter had also been paid by the WE Charity.

How is it that our politicians can skate away so easily from ethics violations? The answer rests with *The Conflict of Interest Act* (2006), a loosely written document with plenty of room to bob and weave around the requirements. As for Mr. Trudeau's family getting paid by the WE Charity, section 11(2) of the act reads: *a public office holder or member of his or her family may accept a gift or other advantage that is received as a normal expression of courtesy or protocol.* Section 11 (3) says that gifts in excess of $1000 shall be forfeited to the Crown, *unless otherwise determined by the Commissioner.* If one's mother getting huge speaking fees is a normal expression of courtesy, then all I have to say is, how utterly sad.

Section 13(2) of the Act reads: *no official shall have an interest in a corporation that is a party to a contract with a public sector entity under which the corporation receives a benefit.* This is the SNC Lavalin situation. But section 13 (3) goes on to note that none of this applies: *if the Commissioner is of the opinion that the contract or interest is unlikely to affect the exercise of the official powers, duties, and functions.* In other words, Mario Dion, the Conflict of Interest and Ethics Commissioner has a whole lot of wiggle room.

As the Commissioner is conducting his investigation, Section 43 (a) reads: *the Commissioner can provide confidential advice to the Prime Minister with respect to the application of this Act.* Section 44(7) reads: *The Commissioner shall provide the Prime Minister with a report setting out the facts in question as well as the Commissioner's analysis and conclusions in relation to the request.* All I have to wonder is, whether the report is edited or revised as the Commissioner and Prime Minster are looking at the report?

If the Commissioner does take action, Section 52 states: *Every public office holder who contravenes the provisions commits a violation and is liable to an administrative monetary penalty not exceeding $500.* How's that for a gentle slap on the wrist? Sad, utterly sad, is all I have to say.

All sarcasm aside, the *Conflict of Interest Act (2006)* looks like a flimsy document. One set of rules for those who we elect to govern us and one set of rules for the rest of us. Is this really how a government should act? Is this what is best for Canadians? Our leaders should be setting better examples as to what is right and what is not right. Is this the kind of leadership that will make Canada a better country? When we get a parking ticket, do we meet with City Hall to negotiate a reduced payment? When we get a speeding ticket, do we meet with the Police Chief to look for a way around making the ticket stick? How about thieves who commit a crime?

What are your thoughts on the idea that our society is breaking into two halves: those with means and privilege, and the rest of us? Is this the society you want your grand kids to grow up in? Now that you know about the Hockey Canada scandal, do you want to see your children playing hockey? What are your thoughts on the data leaks from the offshore law firms? Now that you know Canada is gaining a reputation as a tax haven itself, do you feel discouraged every time you get a paycheque and see taxes deducted? How do you feel about elected officials bobbing and weaving around ethics violations? Are you now asking yourself—what is going on?

CHAPTER 5

Canada is not alone in having elite personalities behave like they have a different set of rules. My grandson will surely read in the history books about an individual who exploited the desire of certain elites who wanted to march to their own tune. That individual was Jeffrey Epstein.

Jeffrey Epstein had a knack for befriending elite personalities; for taking their money, for giving them access to sexual experiences with young girls. How he did this will be the subject of discussion for a long time to come. The elites are not talking. Neither is Epstein. He died in his cell at Rikers Island prison in New York. Apparently, the guards were looking the other way when it all happened.

Epstein owned a private island in the Bahamas where he would take his clients. The mode of transport was his private plane, nicknamed the "Lolita Express." Epstein had a helper—Ghislaine Maxwell, daughter of disgraced British newspaper magnate Robert Maxwell.

The story of Robert Maxwell is fascinating. He was born Jan Ludvik Hyman Binyamin Hoch in Czechoslovakia in 1923. He escaped his native country and ended up in Britain where he served in the British military during World War II. After the War, he ventured into the publishing industry with Pergamon Press. He dabbled with politics, serving in the 1960s as a Labour Party MP. He eventually bought into the newspaper business. But his flamboyant lifestyle all fell apart in 1989. Banks called his loans and he sold assets to try to stay afloat. In 1991, his body was found floating in the water near his yacht and authorities concluded he had fallen overboard. Further to the family drama, as his estate was settled, authorities learned he had raided the pension plans of the various newspaper companies he had purchased.

Daughter Ghislaine fled to New York City where she eventually met Jeffrey Epstein. The two hit it off quickly; Ghislaine needed money to support the lifestyle she felt entitled to and Epstein needed an operative who would find young girls and groom them for his clients. Epstein would then use his suave social skills and connections to find elite personalities who were craving sex with young girls. He would make the connection, in exchange for money. Lots of it.

One of the elites who was photographed in 2001 at Epstein's New York townhouse with his arm around a young girl was none other than Prince Andrew, Duke of York, Earl of Inverness, Baron Killyleagh, ex-husband of Sarah Ferguson, father of Beatrice and Eugenie. The girl was Virginia Roberts.

All was well. Until Ms. Roberts decided to tell all. It was a bombshell. Prince Andrew took to the media to clear his name. During a BBC interview, he insisted he had done nothing wrong. As for the 2001 pictures, he said the pictures were forged.

Virginia Roberts' association with Epstein goes back to 2001. Ghislaine Maxwell was spending time at Donald Trump's (yes, that Donald Trump) Mara Lago estate. Maxwell got to know Roberts, who was working as a spa attendant. In 2002, Maxwell sent Roberts to a massage training school in Thailand. While in Thailand, she met Robert Guiffre. The two went to Australia where they got married, settled down, and decided to start a family. Virginia Roberts was now Virginia Guiffre.

Back in the US, evidence started to leak about Epstein. Police gathered details for a criminal case. The police located Virginia Guiffre in Australia and solicited her help, which she decided to give. In 2009, she launched a lawsuit against Epstein detailing how Maxwell had recruited her into a life of sex trafficking. The case was settled out of court for $500,000.

By August 2019, authorities had compiled enough evidence to charge Epstein. The FBI met his private plane as it flew into a New York airport and they took Epstein into custody. Strangely enough, days later Epstein was found dead in his cell. Stranger yet, the guards on duty had not seen or heard anything. It is obvious that Epstein in a prison cell was a ticking timebomb. As the old adage goes, loose lips sink ships. Who else had he taken money from? In July 2020, Maxwell was found hiding in a farmhouse in New Hampshire and was also arrested. She has subsequently been tried and sentenced to 20 years in prison. She will get out when she is 81 years old, if she lives that long.

In August 2021, Virginia Guiffre initiated a lawsuit against Prince Andrew, alleging sexual assault and intentional infliction of emotional distress. In the end, an out of court settlement was reached (rumoured to be in the area of $10 million).

This entire episode has left an indelible stain on the British royals. Andrew has been stripped of all his titles and appointments. He is no longer a working member of the Royal family. In late 2022, rumors began to swirl that Andrew was contemplating a move to the tiny Kingdom of Bahrain. Andrew has known King Sheikh Hamad bin Isa Al Khalifah for some time. The Kingdom of Bahrain conveniently has no extradition treaty with Britain or the US. Would a move to Bahrain leave Andrew free to continue his dalliances with young girls? One can only speculate. Maybe, though, the whole Epstein affair will serve as a stark reminder to these elites that they cannot march to their own drumbeat. They cannot just do what they want with whom they want, when they want.

CHAPTER 6

When I was growing up on the farm, my mother always had a picture of the Queen sitting on the shelf above where the telephone was mounted to the wall. The rebellious streak in me caused me to question why the royal family was so important. On more than one occasion, the sting of the yardstick connecting with my rear reminded me that my questions were out of line.

The history of royalty goes back centuries. The various European nations all had royalty in the form of Kings and Queens. In the aftermath of the decline of the Roman Empire, some families who had enjoyed a connection to the Roman Empire swiftly moved to acquire land that had once belonged to the Empire. With their acquired land came power and influence and the ability to amass armies. Attacks would be carried out against other families of means and influence. To the victor would go the spoils of war. Some families grew to be very powerful and surrounded themselves with advisors, both religious and military. The families of influence had children who married the children of other wealthy

European families. Through strategic marriage, spheres of influence were expanded.

Consider for example, the collection of lands in the Saxe Coburg & Gotha region of Germany. The first Duke of the Saxe Coburg & Gotha region was Ernest I. Ernest's second son Albert married his first cousin Victoria. Victoria's father was Prince Edward, the fifth child of King George III. Victoria's mother was Victoria, Princess of the Saxe Coburg-Saalfeld. Their offspring married the offspring of other European families, solidifying and extending their power and influence. After World War I, with anti-German sentiment running strong, the family changed its name to the House of Windsor. Their sphere of influence has remained intact over the years. In 2022, the head of the House of Windsor died. Her name was Queen Elizabeth II. She was succeeded by her eldest son Charles who now calls himself King Charles III.

Russia had royalty, the Czars. There is one figure in Russian royalty that demonstrates that sometimes the ruling elite can be downright nasty. That figure is Ivan IV, more commonly known as Ivan the Terrible. Ivan's father, Vasili the Grand Prince of Moscow, died when Ivan was three years old. His mother passed away when he was eight. The young Ivan soon found himself in a tug of war between two elite families, the Shuiskys and Beleskys. Although he had technically taken over the reins of power from his father, they tried to influence young Ivan and even treated him poorly. Something inside Ivan snapped. He started taking out his hatred on animals. He would pull feathers from live birds. He would throw dogs and cats from upper-storey windows. By 1453, the Shuisky family had shoved aside the Belesky family in a nasty power struggle. All that remained now was to get Ivan out of the way. But they underestimated the angry young man. Without warning, he suddenly ordered the most senior member of the Shuisky family arrested and put to death.

In 1558-1560, Ivan waged war to conquer the neighbouring state of Lithuania. He appointed his good friend, nobleman Prince Kurbsky to lead the troops. But Kurbsky turned tail, defecting to the Lithuanian side and, with help from Poland and Sweden, led at attack on Russia. Ivan was pissed. No longer could he trust the nobility. He created an entity called Oprichnina, a secret police organization with unlimited power. Any nobleman who irked Ivan would be tortured and killed. Ivan's favourite execution methods included boiling alive, impalement on a stick, roasting over an open fire, or being torn limb from limb by wild horses. In 1570, Ivan became convinced that the city of Novgorod was out to get him. He ordered a full assault of the city. Bureaucrats, merchants, priests, monks, and prominent citizens were rounded up. They were tortured and executed; many were roasted alive in specially constructed large frying pans. Ivan's Oprichniki men rounded up women and children and tossed them into the Volkhov River. Their heads were held underwater until they were dead. By the time Ivan and his Oprichniki were done, it is estimated that 12,000 people had been killed. Ivan died of a stroke at the age of 54 while playing chess.

It is my hope that my grandsons both take the time to read about the ruling elite families that dominated Europe. It is my hope that my grandsons come to understand that it was wealth and land holdings that gave these families their power and elevated status. This status then inevitably led to some form of government control.

When I was a kid growing up in rural Saskatchewan, I would sometimes hear the expression "blue blood." Now that I see how these elite families intermarried, people marrying their cousins, I understand the expression. It is unfortunate that the school system did not comprehensively teach us about the evolution of these elite families. All we were ever told was that we had to pay homage to the royals. I remember asking a teacher in school why only the son or daughter of the queen can only inherit this position. Usually, the answers over the years were along the lines of "It's tradition" or "They are important." Talk about garbage answers.

I taught my children as they were growing up that no one is any better than they are. As I think back, I wish I could again be in that one-room schoolhouse where a teacher told me that someone is better than me. Someone who has risen to wealth because of some fictitious notion that they have royal blood. I would confront that teacher and ask, "What the hell are you talking about?"

Canada's connection to British royalty raises the issue of the Governor General. The Constitution Act of 1867 provides for a Governor General to act as the Queen's representative in Ottawa. Consider what sections 9,10, and 11 of the Constitution Act state:

Section 9: The Executive Government and Authority of and over Canada is hereby declared to continue and be vested in the Queen.

Section 10: The Provisions of this Act referring to the Governor General extend and apply to the Governor General of Canada, carrying on the Government of Canada on behalf and in the Name of the Queen.

In addition, the Act provides for a group of advisors to assist with running the country.

Section 11: There shall be a Council to aid and advise in the Government of Canada, and the persons who are to be members of that Council shall be from time to time chosen and summoned by the Governor General and sworn in as Privy Councillors, and members thereof may be from time to time removed by the Governor General.

The Governor General is the Queen's representative. The Governor General is appointed by the Queen upon the advice of the Prime Minister.

The Governor General has always been handsomely rewarded. Records show that in 1959, Major General Georges Vanier who was Governor General at the time was earning $48,666. Some financial math that assumes an average annual inflation rate of 3.1% says that today that Governor General would be earning $343,000. In actual fact, the Governor General in 2023 will be paid $342,100. The question I grapple with is, why do we have to pay the Governor General so much money?

Now, let's dance with populist politics. Consider the 2017 appointment of Julie Payette to the Governor General position. Highly educated. Female. Military experience. Mission Control specialist. Crew member on the 1999 Discovery Shuttle mission. What's not to like? Here is what rips me up. Her appointment to the Governor General position came with a $290,000 salary. And then, she turned out not to be the leader that many thought she would be. She resigned on January 21, 2021, following a workplace review that concluded she had belittled, berated, and publicly humiliated Rideau Hall staff and created a toxic, verbally abusive workplace. Wow! That's what $290,000 per year buys! And now dear taxpayer, it's time to pony up. Ms. Payette will, for the rest of her life, receive a $150,000 per year pension. What a farce! What a joke!

And how are these benefits calculated? The *Governor General Act of 1985* tells all. The pension annuity will be 1/3 of what the Governor General was paid in 1967 adjusted for inflation. Let's do some math. In 1967 the Governor General was earning a salary $48,666. Taking 1/3 of this amount and then applying some financial math that assumes an average annual inflation rate of 4% says that today a retiring Governor General would get $146,000. In actual fact, the number is $150,000.

As for the supplementary benefits, in 1952 the Governor General was paid $100,000 in benefits. Applying some financial math that assumes an average annual inflation rate of just under 2% says that today a retiring Governor General would get a supplement of $220,000. In actual fact, the number is $206,000. This calculation is dictated by something called the *Supplementary Retirement Benefits Act (1985)*.

After Ms. Payette's departure, Prime Minister Trudeau had to scramble to find a replacement. He appointed Mary Simon as Canada's new Governor General. Her annual salary is $302,114 plus expenses. Who is Mary Simon? She was born in northern Quebec. Her dad worked for the local Hudson's Bay outpost. Her mom was a local Inuk girl. Her parents raised her in the traditional Inuit lifestyle. From an early age she learned how to hunt, fish, sew Inuit clothing, and travel by dog sled. From 1969 to 1973, she worked as a producer and announcer for CBC Radio's Northern Service. She also taught the Inuktitut language at McGill University. She eventually realized that her calling in life would be advocating for the Arctic and for the Inuit who lived there. She was elected to the Northern Quebec Inuit Association Board of Directors. It was this Board that helped arrive at the James Bay and Northern Quebec Agreement in 1975; at $120 million, the largest land settlement to that time in Canadian history. She next found herself elected as the vice-president of the Makivik Corporation, the entity set up to administer the $120 million of settlement money. This management position provided her with a seat at first ministers meetings and she was even present at the negotiations leading to the Charlottetown Accord. In 1994, she was appointed by Prime Minister Jean Chrétien to be Canadian Ambassador for Circumpolar Affairs. Her political trajectory was pretty much set after that.

Sure, I get it. After the Payette fiasco, Mr. Trudeau needed someone who had some political skills; who could get the job done without rocking the boat. Mary Simon was a natural fit. Plus, her Indigenous ancestry would dovetail nicely with the politics surrounding that subject. But here is what pisses me off to no end. No sooner did she get settled into the job that she decided she had to go to Expo 2020 in Dubai. Actually, the originally scheduled 2020 event was postponed to early 2022 due to COVID. This junket cost the Canadian taxpayer a cool $93,117.89. Oh, and that was just for food and drink. No, she could not travel alone. She had to drag an entourage of 29 others along for the ride; feeding and watering them along the way. The total bill for this bullshit adventure was a stunning $1,307,731.39!

What is the message that this Expo junket sends? What are the optics? This farce says, hello Canada, we—your leaders, just don't give a shit. We know that many Canadian families are having a difficult time paying their mortgages, putting food on the table for their kids, paying for gas for the vehicle. We couldn't give a rat's ass about you. We can do what we want, spend what we want, travel where we want, and the rest of you can go to hell. We are important people. So, suck it up!

But, as far as I am concerned, there is a limit to how far you can push the average person. There is a limit to what a person will endure. In 1917, as World War I was coming to a close, Russia was ruled by Czar Nicholas II. His wife was Alexandra Feodorovna, Princess Alix of Hesse. She was also Queen Victoria's granddaughter. Alix held the Russian people in contempt and was difficult to get along with in nobility circles. World War I had been a tipping point for Alix. When Russia went to war against Germany, Alix with her German heritage became hugely unpopular. When Czar Nicholas made the decision to go to the front lines to be with his troops, he left Alix in charge. She soon aligned herself with a strange character called Rasputin. Alix soon found herself being accused of conspiracy with Germany. As Russia struggled in the war effort, it became difficult to even get food supplies by rail into Russia towns and cities. Hungry people will resort to whatever it takes to survive. When Nicholas returned from the front lines, he and Alix and their children were placed under house arrest. He appealed to his cousin George V for safe passage to Britain. "Nothing doing," said George who was concerned about hanging onto his wealth and power. The situation steadily grew worse. In July 1918, the family was summarily executed and their bodies buried in the nearby woods. The people had spoken.

Another story of people becoming unhappy to the point of taking action comes from France in the late 1700s. Debt levels were rising, the economy was slowing, taxation was unfairly applied, food prices were rising, wages were not keeping pace, agricultural methods were inefficient and outdated, the population had surged, and the ruling elite class just did not grasp the frustration of the people. Instead of focusing on domestic issues, the French government instead had opted for strategies such as borrowing money with which to support the American independence movement.

French society at the time was divided into three *estates*: the clergy (First Estate), the nobility (Second Estate), and the common man (Third Estate). In January 1789, King Louis XVI, exercised his royal powers. He summoned the representatives of all three Estates to a meeting in Paris. Louis promised that he was going to fix the problems that were dogging France. The last time the *estates* had met in one place had been 175 years prior. Things had changed; but Louis was unaware. What had been senior clergy and nobility, had devolved into something less.

The First Estate had 303 delegates, over half of whom were now ordinary parish priests. The Second Estate had 282 delegates, about one-third of whom were just minor land owners. The Third Estate had 578 delegates, half of whom were lawyers, and one-third of whom were tradesmen, not commoners. As the meetings got underway, the Third Estate demanded that all delegates be treated equally and given one vote. Louis coldly dismissed this idea. The delegates of the Third Estate then announced they were calling themselves the *National Assembly*, an assembly not of nobility, but of the common man. As Louis dug his heels into the mud further, the members of the Second Estate decide to join with the members of the Third Estate. As this confusing situation evolved, Louis tried closing various buildings in Paris where the delegates could meet. When this news circulated, people in the streets erupted in anger. On July 14, 1789 mobs of angry people attacked the Bastille, destroying the fortress prison in short order. To this day, July 14 each year is celebrated as *Bastille Day.*

The unrest spread quickly. Even the newly declared National Assembly spiraled down into disagreements. Something had to happen, and fast. On August 4, the Assembly declared an end to feudalism, whereby privileges held by the nobility would no longer be observed. People would be treated equally before the law; anyone could now run for public office. Even the concept of mandatory tithes to the Church was discarded. But more had to be done before society completely broke down.

On October 5, 1789, a crowd of women convened outside the Paris City Hall. They demanded lower prices and an increased supply of bread. They broke into the City Hall and took the cache of weapons they found stored inside. Weapons in hand, 7,000 women marched on Versailles. They entered the Assembly Hall and began to state their demands. To this day, this event is known as the *October March* or *October Days*. News of the women's march fired up the protestors in the streets. People stormed the Royal apartments, searching for Marie Antoinette, but she had fled. She and Louis were eventually located and were placed under house arrest in the Tuileries Palace.

On January 17, 1793, the Assembly condemned Louis to death; the charge being conspiracy against public liberty and general safety. Four days later, Louis and Marie were taken to the Place de la Concord. The guillotine did the rest of the work. The people had spoken.

Do the stories of citizens in 1918 Russia and in 1789 France tell us that all monarchies eventually run their course and the common man rises?

CHAPTER 7

One set of rules for those of means and privilege. Light taps on the wrist for ethics violations. Top officials spending money with an I-don't-give-a-shit attitude. I am afraid of the potential for our own elected officials taking a heavier handed approach to running the country.

In March 2020, a virus flared up in Wuhan, China. It soon earned the name COVID-19. Viruses are nothing new. The human animal occupies the planet alongside biological viruses and bacteria. Think back in history and you will soon realize that mankind has had its fair share of run-ins with biological viruses. In the mid-1300s, illness flared up in central Asia. It was caused by the bacteria *Yersinia pestis*, found in small mammals and their fleas. A human coming into contact with these fleas and getting flea-bitten would soon develop swollen, infected lymph nodes. Death was sure to follow. The flea worked its way across Asia, into the Crimean region, north Africa, and finally Europe. Between 1347 and 1351, millions of people died. As quickly as it started, it seemingly went away. But I believe it was not gone; just dormant.

Between 1600 and 1670, over 2.5 million people across Europe died when the bacteria made a return visit. Governments in those days made infected people isolate in their homes. Ships coming into ports would sit at anchor for weeks to ensure the crew was free of disease. As quickly as it came, it left again; or so it seemed.

A third wave of the bacterial infection began in southern China in 1865. It eventually found its way to Hong Kong. With so many ships coming and going from Hong Kong, the bacteria soon spread farther, finding its way to India. Over 12 million people died in a 20-year span of time.

In 1918, another wave of illness struck mankind. This illness earned the name *Spanish Flu*, although it had little to do with Spain. It was caused by the *H1N1* virus and was thought to have originated in birds. During the two years that it spread around the world, some 50 million people died. People were encouraged to isolate, avoid large gatherings, wear a mask, and practice good hygiene. There was little else to do.

The pattern throughout history seems clear. Isolate, avoid, sanitize. But that pattern would be upended with the appearance of COVID-19. As the disease began to spread, a complete shit-show erupted. Donald Trump, the President of the United States, took an unusual stance. He promoted the belief that the illness was not to be believed. He fought against public health policy efforts to contain the spread. The United States became horribly divided; governors and politicians siding with Trump decided they would not be doing much to prevent the disease from spreading. Governors and politicians who were of the opposite political stripe supported public health measures of masking and isolating to prevent the spread.

As the political wrangling intensified, people were dying from COVID-19. It seemed everyone had a different statistic for deaths. And that is when conspiracy theories started to mount. It was Bill Gates. It was the New World Order. It was Klaus Schwab. It was China trying to destroy the world. People who thought COVID-19 was a hoax started claiming the death statistics were fake. At one point in late 2021, nearly 1000 people per day in the USA were dying from COVID. Stories soon circulated that a person dying in hospital for whatever cause were listed as having died from COVID. It was a no-win situation.

What people failed to look at was the basic data. I am not at all surprised that people either did not look at the data or could not decipher the data. Our public-school systems stopped teaching critical thinking skills years ago. People can no longer think. This seems to especially ring true for the recent generations who grew up with the internet. When confronted with a situation like COVID-19, people instinctively took to the closest search engine algorithm looking for answers.

The National Center for Health Statistics has been tracking annual death totals in the US since 1920. Their annual number includes deaths from all causes; car accidents to cancer to old age. A death is a death is a death. From 1920 through 2019, the annual death totals have been an upsloping line on a chart. The percentage of the population dying each year in the US is just shy of 0.85%. But, in 2020 and into 2022 that relatively constant upslope steepened. The annual death rate rose to just over 1% of the population. That is about a 17% increase. Instead of 7,000 people a day dying in the US, the number was now around 8,000 a day. Not only were people dying from COVID, they were dying from conditions that could not be appropriately or quickly treated due to the priority focus on COVID patients and general health care system closures. In Canada, during the worst of the COVID outbreak, statistics show an excess number of deaths of 53,700. A hoax? Fake? New World Order? Maybe. But the point is, more people were suddenly dying in North America and COVID was the only new variable in the equation. Do the math!

Pharma companies Moderna, BioNTek, and Pfizer rushed to develop an mRNA vaccine. Politicians and health regulators rushed to approve the vaccines for human use. The subject of microbiology is a complex one. And of course, we don't teach microbiology to any great extent in our public education system. (On that note, I sincerely hope that my grandsons have the opportunity to learn something about microbiology; even if they have to read basic textbooks and teach themselves.) Understanding how the cells in the human body work is one of the most valuable areas of information a person can learn. In the case of the COVID, the vaccine was designed to trigger the human body cells to generate a protein substance. Immune cells in the body would recognize this protein as an invader and move to develop antigens to kill off the protein. Once the human body had these antigens, the immune system would be able to fight off the COVID virus.

New stuff? Not exactly. Scientists have been exploring mRNA technology for the past couple decades, beginning in 1987 at the Salk Institute for Biological Studies in La Jolla, California. However, an uninformed population with no understanding of microbiology in the midst of a rising death rate is not the ideal target audience for introducing a new vaccine to be administered by way of an intramuscular jab. What the mRNA vaccines did was divide the country. Arguments erupted within families. People who were against the concept of having government dictate that vaccination was mandatory turned against people who were in favour of vaccination. Some companies mandated that their employees had to get vaccinated. Employees opposed to vaccinations up and quit their jobs. Airlines required vaccinations before a person could fly. Only vaccinated people could get into restaurants. Travel to the USA required proof of full vaccination. It was a shit-show the likes of which may never be seen again.

One thing that COVID and mRNA vaccines did accomplish was sow the seeds for deeper government mistrust. Prior to COVID, governments implemented laws that they felt were in the best interest of society. People often reacted with mild disgust; with a hint of mistrust. Highway speed limits were implemented. Seatbelts in vehicles became a standard requirement. People had to pay new taxes. Over the years, as governments implemented new policies, some people grumbled and bitched. Others accepted new government policies and laws. Every now and again, the people would speak. Democracy would assert itself. The ruling political party would be voted out of office. A new party with a fresh slate of promises would take up office. Society kept moving forward. Life went on.

But the vaccine issue was a tipping point. From here on, government mistrust stands to only grow bigger and become more widespread. This was almost predictable. Government cannot mandate that people accept a needle in the arm, especially when those same people lack the basic scientific knowledge to understand what is in the syringe and how the contents of that syringe will interact with the body's cells. Government officials spending without restraint or displaying unethical behavior is one thing, government mandating vaccines is quite another. Government heavy-handedness indeed. The questions that will be debated for years to come will be: how could vaccinated people still get COVID? If an unvaccinated person got COVID, was it worse than if they had been vaccinated?

My fear goes even further. The *Canadian Constitution Act (1982)* is what gives all of us protection from this heavy handedness. I believe the mandates initiated by the federal government throughout the COVID crisis have been unconstitutional. The government has not expressed or conducted itself in alignment with the values and practices of a free and democratic society.

Part 1, sections 2,6,7, and 15 of the Constitution are critically important. These are our rights in our democracy.

Section 2 provides for: (a) freedom of conscience and religion, (b) freedom of thought, belief, opinion and expression, including freedom of the press and other media of communication, (c) freedom of peaceful assembly, and (d) freedom of association.

Section 6 provides for: (1) Every citizen of Canada has the right to enter, remain in and leave Canada, (2) Every citizen of Canada and every person having the status of a permanent resident of Canada has the right (a) to move to and take up residence in any province, and (b) to pursue the gaining of a livelihood in any province.

Section 7 provides for: Everyone having the right to life, liberty and security of the person and the right not to be deprived thereof except in accordance with the principles of fundamental justice.

Section 15 provides for: Every individual being equal before and under the law and having the right to the equal protection and equal benefit of the law without discrimination based on race, national or ethnic origin, colour, religion, sex, age or mental or physical disability.

If this all sounds like legal mumbo-jumbo to you, again let me be very clear. Take the time to read the *Canadian Constitution Act*. Better yet, read it with your kids. This document is all that stands between we the people and absolute tyranny. This document defines our rights in our democracy.

Here is what really gets me foaming at the mouth. In January 2022, the Trudeau government mandated that non-essential workers, including truckers coming back from the USA, had to be fully vaccinated. If they were not fully vaccinated, they would be subject to a 14-day quarantine. At this point, COVID had been front and center in people's lives for almost two years. People were getting tired of it all. Every day in the media … COVID, COVID, COVID. The Trudeau trucker vaccination mandate was the proverbial straw that broke the camel's back. In no time at all, pissed off truckers turned their rigs east and started heading to Ottawa. They were going to deliver a message to Ottawa. The Freedom Convoy was on its way.

Initially, people thought a small contingent of truckers would arrive in Ottawa, express their displeasure, and then move on. What happened next made international headlines. The truckers arrived, and they stayed. The streets of downtown Ottawa were choked with rigs, drivers, and people who showed up in support of it all. The Ottawa Police was swamped. The City of Ottawa was paralyzed. The nightly news carried images of truckers sitting in portable hot tubs on Ottawa streets. It was a huge protest the likes of which Canada had never seen before. And then it spread. A convoy of truckers arrived at the Ambassador Bridge in Windsor and set up a blockade. Another group arrived at the border crossing by Coutts, Alberta and set up a blockade. Something had to be done.

What ended up getting done will be debated by legal and Constitutional scholars for decades to come. Prime Minister Trudeau invoked the *Emergency Measures Act* on February 14, 2022. He said, "It is now clear that there are serious challenges to law enforcement's ability to effectively enforce the law. It is no longer a lawful protest at a disagreement over government policy. It is now an illegal occupation. It's time for people to go home." He added, "This is about keeping Canadians safe, protecting people's jobs and restoring confidence in our institutions."

Law enforcement swooped in. Trucks were seized. Bank accounts of the protest's leaders were frozen. Even some people who had sent money on-line to help fund the convoy found their bank accounts frozen. Commenting on the situation, Mr. Trudeau said, "Freedom of expression, assembly and association are cornerstones of democracy, but Nazi symbolism, racist imagery and desecration of war memorials are not." If the Covid vaccine requirements had sowed the seeds of government contempt and mistrust, the invoking of the *Emergency Measures Act* caused those seeds to germinate and start growing. People started talking loudly. Is this the Canada we built? Is this the Canada we worked so hard to create? Is this what we want in our political leadership?

But there was a wrinkle in the fabric. The House of Commons still had to approve the implementation of the Act. On February 21, in a rare weekend sitting, the House of Commons passed the Act in a vote of 185 to 151. Getting to this point required some political bobbing and weaving for Mr. Trudeau because he was sitting on a minority government with 160 seats. A majority in the House of Commons would be 170 seats. Trudeau needed 10 more votes. There was no way he would ever get them from the Conservatives. The Bloc Quebecois was also a no go. Memories in Quebec run deep from way back in 1972 when Pierre Trudeau implemented the *War Measures Act* in response to the FLQ crisis. To get over the 170-vote threshold, Justin Trudeau turned to NDP leader Jagmeet Singh. Singh took the opportunity to make some political hay.

Who is Jagmeet Singh? Jagmeet Singh "Jimmy" Dhaliwal, was born on January 2, 1979 in Scarborough, Ontario. He was the eldest of three children born to his mother, Harmeet Kaur, and his father, Jagtaran Singh, a psychiatrist. When he was one year old, Singh was sent to his family's native Punjab, India, to live with his grandparents. At the time, his mother and father were struggling to make ends meet. His mother, Harmeet, was working in a bank, while father Jagtaran was working as a security guard while studying for his medical recertification. He had trained as a physician in India but had to qualify to practise in Canada.

Baby Jagmeet was eventually reunited with his parents who moved St. John's, Newfoundland, so that his father could attend Memorial University. Jagmeet's sister, Manjot, and brother, Gurratan, were born in Newfoundland. Jagmeet learned English in Newfoundland. To his fellow playmates, he was known as "Jimmy."

When Jagmeet was seven, his family moved to Windsor, Ontario, where his father started to practice medicine. His father sent him to the private Detroit Country Day School in the United States, across the river from Windsor. After high school, Jagmeet attended Western University where he earned a Bachelor of Science degree in biology. He was then accepted into Osgoode Hall Law School in Toronto. After law school, he began working as a criminal defence lawyer in Brampton, Ontario. He soon developed a reputation for doing volunteer legal work for social justice groups. He also helped immigrants and refugees with rights claims. He even visited university campuses in Ontario to give free legal seminars to students.

Moved by the social injustices he was seeing in southern Ontario, Jagmeet decided to take a run at politics. He ran for the federal NDP in the May 2011 election in the riding of Bramalea-Gore-Malton. Jagmeet came close to winning the seat, falling short by just 539 votes. The party's leader was the hugely popular Jack Layton and the 2011 election saw the NDPs seat count in the House of Commons rise from 36 to 103.

Although disappointed at losing, Jagmeet did not back down. In October 2011, he ran in the Ontario provincial election in the Bramalea-Gore-Malton riding. This time he won. It was off to Queen's Park and the Ontario legislature. With his red BMW Z4M coupe, folding bike, tailored suits, and colourful turbans, he quickly became one of the most recognizable MPPs in the legislature.

He soon learned what it meant to hold the balance of power. The Ontario Premier was Kathlene Wynne, but her Liberal Party was in a minority position. In 2013, Jagmeet made a move. He introduced a motion to force Premier Wynne's minority government to reduce private vehicle insurance premiums by 15 per cent. Premier Wynne agreed to the motion. It was that or her government would fall. Jagmeet Singh now had his first taste of power.

The June 2014 election did not go so well for the Ontario NDP. The Party lost seats and as the dust settled, the NDP were in third place in the legislature. However, Jagmeet Singh had managed to get re-elected. He turned his sights to arguing for an end to the police practice of random spot checks, known as *carding* that were unfairly used to target visible minorities.

Meanwhile, in Ottawa the NDP was suffering. Leader Jack Layton had died just after the 2011 election. Quebec MP Thomas Mulcair had been appointed the new leader. But he was no Jack Layton and the popularity of the Party declined.

In the 2015 federal election, the NDP lost 51 seats. Leader Mulcair was shown the exit door in 2016. The stage was now set for a new leader to come in to pick up the pieces. In May 2017, Jagmeet launched his bid for the leadership. His platform included a plan to decriminalize several illegal drugs, a plan to ban racial profiling by the RCMP, and a pledge to reform Canada's electoral system. The popularity that had delivered him to the Ontario legislature spilled over into the leadership contest. Jagmeet Singh took 53% of the ballots on the first vote and the federal NDP had a new leader.

But controversy almost immediately started to swirl. He quickly locked horns with the Quebec government and Bill 62 designed to ban Muslim women from giving or receiving public services while wearing a face covering. He next drew fire when he refused to specifically condemn Sikhs who revere and display posters of Talwinder Singh Parmar, the reputed mastermind of the 1985 Air India bombing that killed 329 people. He next had a falling out with Alberta NDP Premier Rachel Notley. Ms. Notley was in favour of the Trans Mountain Pipeline expansion project. British Columbia NDP Premier John Horgan was opposed. After sitting on the fence for a while, Jagmeet announced his opposition to the project. Not exactly the news Premier Notley wanted to hear from the new federal NDP leader.

In August 2018, NDP MP Kennedy Stewart resigned his Burnaby South seat so he could throw his hat in the ring for the Vancouver mayoralty election. Jagmeet announced that he would run in the Burnaby South by-election. He won handily. He could now take a seat in the House of Commons in Ottawa.

Leading into the 2019 federal election, Jagmeet unveiled a wide-ranging platform dubbed the *New Deal for People*. The platform called for a national pharmacare program, an end to subsidies for gas and oil companies, tighter emissions targets, expanded cell coverage, caps on Internet and cell phone bills, more affordable housing, and better living conditions for First Nations, Inuit and Métis communities. To help pay for these plans, the platform proposed increased corporate taxes and a new 1% wealth tax on fortunes over $20 million.

During the campaign, Jagmeet demonstrated his poise during the televised debates. He had to be on his best behavior with all the controversy that he had been generating. He likely sensed that the NDP was in trouble. The pollsters were indicating so. His political survival skills kicked in. As the campaign entered its final throes, pictures of Justin Trudeau wearing blackface surfaced in the media. Jagmeet could have pounced. He could have gone for the jugular vein. But instead, he took the safe road. Looking at the blackface photos, he waxed prophetically about racism issues. When the votes were tallied, the Liberals had lost ground and so too had the NDP who lost 20 seats. The Liberals had 157 seats, the Conservatives 121 seats, the NDP 24 seats, the Bloc Quebecois 32 seats, and the Green Party had 3 seats. It was another Liberal minority and Jagmeet Singh was once again in the role of king maker.

2021 saw another federal election. Once again, the Liberals failed in their bid to score a majority. The Liberals ended up with 160 seats, the Conservatives with 119 seats, the NDP with 25 seats, the Bloc with their usual 32 seats and the Green party with 2 seats. Jagmeet Singh was once again in the role of king maker. Shades of his days in the Ontario legislature! As for Mr. Trudeau, he was breathing easy again. Sure, he had a minority, but all he needed to pass any major bits of legislation was 10 more votes to bring the total to 170. And where would he find those 10 votes? Hello, Jagmeet. Hello, friend.

Before I venture deeper, there is one thing that gnaws at me. People in this day and age have no clue how the House of Commons is even structured. In fact, less than 2/3 of eligible voters even bother to get off their arses to go to the polling station at election time. I seriously hope my grandsons grows up to be voting citizens. Voting is our constitutional right—and our responsibility as citizens.

The House of Commons is comprised of 338 members, each of whom represents a geographic portion (a riding) of our country. When we go to the polling station at election time, we are voting for the candidate who will represent us (and our riding) in Ottawa. Unless they declare as an independent, each of the candidates listed on the ballot belongs to a political party. Each of those parties has a leader. After the votes are counted across the country on election night, the Party that wins the most ridings gets to form the government. The leader of that party becomes the Prime Minister. If the winning party gets 170 or more seats, then the party is in a majority situation. Any controversial legislation that it wishes to pass will not have enough votes from the other parties to challenge the proposed bill. If the party with the most seats falls shy of 170, then it is in a minority situation. Now it will have to make nice with some members from another party in order to have the needed 170 votes to pass budgets and other bills. This is where politics gets really interesting.

The overall number of seats in the Commons is based on the population of Canada. Each province is allotted a number of seats based on population. There is a mathematical formula that comes into play. If the population of a province grows, more seats are created. The last time the seat numbers were adjusted was in 2011, under Stephen Harper's Conservative government. At that time, the government added 27 more seats for the three fastest-growing provinces—Ontario, Alberta, and British Columbia. Observing that the population of Quebec had declined, Mr. Harper should have removed one seat from Quebec. Instead, he added three more. His reasoning was that Quebec had 23% of the Canadian population, so should have 23% of the seats in the Commons. What is going on? How does Quebec garner so much attention and power?

Back to the subject at hand: Jagmeet Singh ensured that Mr. Trudeau got the needed votes to pass the *Emergency Measures Act*. And make political hay, he surely did. He said he saw the Prime Minister's decision to turn to the *Emergencies Act* as "proof of a failure of leadership." He added, "The reason why we got to this point is because the Prime Minister let the siege in Ottawa go on for weeks and weeks without actually doing anything about it, allowed the convoy to shut down borders without responding appropriately."

What the hell? Singh gives Trudeau the votes he needs to pass a wickedly powerful piece of legislation that all but squelches the rights and freedoms of Canadians, then in a moment of total hypocrisy, he criticizes Trudeau for passing the bill to begin with.

Interim Conservative Leader Candice Bergen cast no illusions about her position. She accused Trudeau of dividing Canadians. She said, "We've seen the prime minister wedge, divide and stigmatize Canadians he doesn't agree with and by doing so he creates so many barriers in terms of trying to solve this problem." She added, "The prime minister had the opportunity to talk and listen to many he disagreed with and he refused to do so, so this looks like a ham-fisted approach that will have the opposite effect." Conservative MP Pierre Poilievre who was running for the Conservative leadership at the time weighed in, saying, "The way to end the protest and illegal blockades is to remove the mandates." He added, "Real simple. Listen to the science, do what other provinces and countries are doing. End the mandates and restrictions so protesters can get back to their lives and their jobs."

The language in the *Emergency Measures Act* states that it cannot be in force for more than 30 days from the date it is invoked; nine days after it was invoked, Trudeau announced he was suspending it.

But who was responsible for the convoy protest? First on the list was Medicine Hat, Alberta resident, Tamara Lich. She was not the sole organizer of the convoy, but she certainly played a role in the events. In Medicine Hat she worked as a logistics administrator for an oil and gas company. When the federal government implemented Bill C-48 and Bill C-69, Lich started to voice her opinions.

Bill C-48, made law in June 2019, brought into being the *Oil Tanker Moratorium Act*, which prohibits oil tankers that are carrying more than 12,500 metric tons of crude oil from stopping, or unloading crude oil at ports or marine installations located along British Columbia's north coast from the northern tip of Vancouver Island to the Alaska border.

Bill C-69, passed in August 2019, brought into effect some sweeping changes, starting with the launching of the *Impact Assessment Agency of Canada* (IAA). Prior to Bill C-69, resource projects were assessed on their biological and physical impacts on the nearby environment. Under Bill C-69, resource projects would be assessed based on their social, health, and economic factors. These factors can be twisted to include just about anything. For example, suppose a mining project proposes to put construction waste materials in a nearby landfill. Under C-69, regulators can now look at the lifespan of that landfill site. What if it gets full? What are the social impacts? If a resource project creates jobs in a nearby community, regulators can now probe the negative impacts of creating those jobs. What will be the greenhouse gas emissions of the project? What about the social impacts on nearby First Nations groups? C-69 basically opens a can of worms; a barrel of monkeys.

Small wonder then that someone with an activist mindset, like Tamara Lich, got upset. She decided to aim her opinions at the political sphere. She got involved with the Wexit Movement, a vocal group calling for western Canada to separate. She followed the Wexit platform as it became the Wildrose Independence Party of Alberta. She eventually left that group to join the separatist Maverick Party where she served in administrative roles. Lich followed the convoy to Ottawa where she took an active role in day-to-day events. When the *Emergency Measures Act* was triggered, she was charged with mischief, counselling mischief, obstructing police, counselling to obstruct police, counselling intimidation, and intimidation by blocking and obstructing one or more highways. Several weeks later, she was released on bail and ordered to have no contact with other organizers.

Next on the target list was organizer and trucking company operator Chris Barber from Swift Current, Saskatchewan. He became annoyed at the government's stand on vaccinations for truckers and he encouraged truckers from Saskatchewan to get involved in the convoy. In Ottawa, once the *Emergency Measures Act* was implemented, he was charged with counselling to commit mischief, counselling to disobey a court order, and counselling to obstruct police. He was quickly released on bail, but ordered to avoid contact with other organizers, including Tamara Lich.

Next on the list was Alberta resident, Pat King. Mr. King has a history of far-right conspiracy ideas. He had connections to the Wexit Movement, which is likely where he met Tamara Lich. He was arrested in Ottawa, charged with perjury, obstruction of justice, mischief and intimidation, and spent five months in jail before being released on bail.

As the convoy gathered momentum, King, Barber, and Lich realized they needed logistical support to keep the effort organized. They reached out to Ontario resident Tom Marazzo. Mr. Marazzo had recently made headlines when he was fired from his teaching position at Georgian College. The reason for termination was his outspoken opposition to the COVID vaccination. Mr. Marazzo spent 25 years in the Canadian military, earning an engineering technology diploma and an MBA degree along the way. His tactical and strategic advice helped the convoy stay on track. He regularly acted as spokesperson, held news conferences, and engaged in discussions with the Ottawa Police. His professional behavior prevented him from ever being charged.

With Lich and Chris Barber out on bail pending a September 2023 trial date, the situation surrounding the convoy event settled down. But it boiled over again in June 2022 when the Justice Centre for Constitutional Freedoms (JCCF), a legal organization and registered charity based in Calgary, decided that the 2022 recipient of the *George Jonas Freedom Award* would be none other than Tamara Lich. Lawyers for Lich made application to an Ottawa judge to amend her bail terms so that she could travel to Toronto to receive the award. One condition of her bail that the judge did not amend was the clause of no contact with other convoy organizers. To ensure no contact, she was required to have her lawyer present at the awards ceremony. Lich was placed at the awards gala head table, which Tom Marazzo also happened to be at. After delivering a brief acceptance speech at the podium, she walked around the head table, receiving words of congratulations from those seated at the table. She later had a photo taken of her standing next to Tom Marazzo.

No sooner had she returned to Medicine Hat than she was taken into police custody, charged with a breach of bail conditions. After a brief court appearance in Medicine Hat, she was transported back to Ottawa and jail. The wheels of justice can sometimes turn slow. She would spend the next 48 days behind bars while her lawyer Lawrence Greenspon tried to get her in front of a judge. The roadblock, it seemed, was Crown prosecutor Moiz Karimjee. His mindset was that she should remain in jail for having violated one of her bail conditions. But Justice Andrew Goodman pushed back against Karimjee. Justice Goodman reminded Karimjee that Lich's charges were for non-violent crimes and his stance towards her was unwarranted. Justice Goodman released her on the same bail terms as before, except he added a $37,000 surety bond this time. Lich's lawyer, Lawrence Greenspon, commented afterwards, "It's extremely disappointing that she spent this amount of time before she could be released on what the judge described as a tenuous breach of condition and what I would say is a very defensible, minor, and technical alleged breach."

September 2023 will finally see an end to this saga when Lich, King, and Barber will appear at their trial. But really what are their chances of winning?

As for the NDP, the seeds of destruction may also have been sown. With Jagmeet's decision to support the Liberals on the *Emergency Measures Act*, he strayed off script; the NDP core principles had been tossed overboard. If Tommy Douglas were here today, what would he say? (I hope that my grandson will one day read about the political history of Saskatchewan, about the CCF Party, about Tommy Douglas, and about the NDP. The political framework for the CCF and the NDP was a document from 1933 called the *Regina Manifesto*. The overarching goal of the CCF movement was to support the little guy. Tommy Douglas took these principles to heart. He did his best to kick start the Saskatchewan economy after World War II. His crowning achievement was starting Medicare in Saskatchewan. Shortly afterwards, Prime Minister Diefenbaker took the Saskatchewan platform and rolled it out across the entire country. That is why today, if you get ill, the medical system will look after you regardless of how much money you have. Tommy Douglas is regarded as one of the most influential Canadians to have ever lived; a man who devoted hours of his life to the average Canadian worker.)

Jagmeet Singh ignored all of this rich Party history and policy. It was as if he decided to look after himself and his aspirations for re-election over protecting the individual.

Did the Government of Canada go against the value of the Canadian Constitution with its implementation of the *Emergency Measures Act?*

Was it a test? If so, it was a scary test. Politicians of all stripes now know they can implement the Act with relative ease, even if they are a few seats short of a majority. The powers it bestows on law enforcement are monumental. I sincerely hope that my grandsons never see the Act implemented in the future. The next federal election will deliver the verdict for Singh and his Party. The people of Canada will act as judge, jury, and executioner.

CHAPTER 8

Another event that disheartens me is the Omar Khadr affair. Omar Khadr was born September 19, 1986 in Toronto to immigrant parents, father Ahmed Said Khadr from Egypt and mother Maha Elsamnah from Palestine. Ahmed worked for Muslim children's charities in Pakistan and Afghanistan; the family moved a few times between Canada and Pakistan to accommodate Ahmed's work. Ahmed was suspected but never proven to have close connections to Osama bin Laden. Ahmed was arrested in 1995 in Pakistan in connection with a bombing of the Egyptian embassy but was freed a year later. Ahmed later was a suspect in the 9/11 terror attacks in New York and Washington, D.C. In 2002, Omar's father sent his three sons, including Omar, to an al-Qaida training camp in Afghanistan. And that's when things went off the rails. Omar Khadr became a child soldier.

On July 27, 2002, American forces attacked the compound where Khadr and his fellow militants lived. As the American soldiers entered the compound, US Sgt. Christopher Speer was killed by a grenade and Sgt. Layne Morris was blinded in one eye by a grenade explosion. After the bombing and shelling had subsided, Omar Khadr was the only survivor among the militants; he had been shot twice in the back by an American soldier.

He was given medical attention by the US forces and sent to Bagram air force base. Over the next three months, Khadr was interrogated on 40 occasions, sometimes for up to eight hours a day. In the fall of 2002, he was loaded onto an airplane and moved to a prison cell at the US naval base at Guantánamo Bay, Cuba. At the age of 16, Omar Khadr was one of the youngest prisoners ever to be held at Guantánamo. As far as the American military was concerned, Khadr was the one who had thrown the grenades. In the eyes of the American military, he was guilty.

In early 2003, Canadian journalists learned that officials from the Canadian spy agency CSIS had traveled to Guantánamo to interrogate Mr. Khadr. This news caught the attention of Dennis Edney and Nate Whitling, Edmonton-based lawyers who specialize in Constitutional law. Edney and Whitling traveled to Scarborough, Ontario and knocked on the door of Omar Khadr's grandparents. They proposed to take on the Omar Khadr case, pro bono; free of charge.

Edney and Whitling made application to the Federal Court to have the court hear their argument. They argued that CSIS traveling to Guantánamo to privately interrogate Khadr had effectively denied him access to legal counsel and the right to challenge his detention.

As Edney and Whitling assembled their case over the following year, they left no stone unturned. They even found reports compiled by US lawyers who had traveled to Guantánamo in the Fall of 2004 to conduct a tribunal sitting. In September 2004, a *Combatant Status Review Tribunal* at Guantánamo concluded that Khadr was an "enemy combatant." During the tribunal sitting, the US lawyers learned that Khadr had told CSIS about his treatment in Bagram prison and also in Guantánamo. He had told CSIS about long interrogations, arms and legs handcuffed in painful positions, and how he had been used as a human mop to clean up his own urine. He had been beaten, choked, deprived of light, deprived of sleep, and forced into harmful stress positions. Guards had threatened to deport him to Arab countries like Syria where, they claimed, he would be raped by other men.

Stared down by US authorities, CSIS had buckled at the knees and handed the 2003 documented and video-taped interrogation data to the US legal authorities.

In 2004, Khadr's mother and sister agreed to appear in a CBC documentary to talk about his situation. When they expressed pro Al Qaeda sentiment and anti-Canadian sentiment in the documentary, Canadians became aware of the Khadr saga. Few had sympathy for Khadr's situation.

On August 8, 2005, Edney and Whitling won their first major victory. The Federal Court of Canada handed down a temporary injunction prohibiting CSIS from conducting further interrogations of Khadr. Edney and Whitling then made sure the Canadian public were made well aware of Khadr's treatment.

But Edney and Whitling were not done yet. They wanted to get their hands on all of the interrogation data that CSIS had collected. The Federal Court refused. Edney and Whitling appealed. In May 2007, the Federal Court of Appeal agreed with Edney and Whitling and the Court ordered the documents to be released. Not a chance, said the Canadian government, and then appealed the matter to the Supreme Court.

Meanwhile, back in Guantánamo, things were getting worse. In 2006, the US Supreme Court had struck down the Guantanamo *Combatant Status Review Tribunal* model, due to its lack of legal rights. So, Congress pushed back. In 2006, Congress passed a new law, the *Military Commission Act*, which explicitly denied *habeas corpus* rights to Guantanamo detainees. The Act further stated that information obtained under cruel and unusual treatment would be allowed as evidence at hearings. Even the word *torture* was given a makeover. Instead of torture, interrogators were given the right to use an *array of abusive practices*, practically all deemed unlawful by international law. Khadr's charges were then amplified. He was additionally charged with Murder in Violation of the Law of War, Attempted Murder in Violation of the Law of War, Conspiracy, Providing Material Support for Terrorism, and Spying.

In May 2008, the Supreme Court agreed with Edney and Whitling. The Court ruled in favour of Khadr, saying that Canada's participation in

Guantanamo's flawed legal system had brought Canada into violation of international laws. But the Court limited the number of CSIS documents that Edney and Whitling could access. In the end, only a handful of documents from among a collection of thousands of documents were turned over. One of these documents contained evidence that would prove valuable. Edney and Whitling now had written proof that CSIS had been told in no uncertain terms that Khadr had been subjected to severe sleep deprivation, something the American's called "the frequent flyer program." Khadr had apparently been moved every three hours to a different cell. This had gone on for weeks at a time.

A Canadian citizen had been tortured, CSIS knew about it, the Canadian government did nothing to help. On the heels of this document release, Liberal Senator Roméo Dallaire appeared before a foreign affairs committee on international human rights, and argued that Omar Khadr was clearly a child soldier who shouldn't be prosecuted by an illegal court system at Guantanamo Bay. Instead, Dallaire argued that Khadr should be reintegrated into society. He stated, "Canada is heading down a slippery slope by failing to obey the United Nations conventions on child soldiers to which it is a signatory."

Edney and Whitling next launched a lawsuit against the Harper government on behalf of Khadr. They argued that the Canadian government should demand Khadr's release. Meanwhile, US authorities were getting ready to send Khadr to trial in the American court system. In April 2009, the Federal Court of Canada ordered that Khadr be returned to Canadian soil. The victory dance was a short one. The federal government appealed.

In August 2009, the Federal Appeals Court denied the appeal. Harper turned up his nose at the appeal denial and in November 2009, the Canadian government presented its arguments to the Supreme Court.

In January 2010, the Court ruled that Khadr's right to life, liberty and security of person under Section 7 of the *Canadian Charter of Rights and Freedoms* had all been violated. But the Court would not bring Khadr back to Canadian soil. Meanwhile, in the US, Attorney General Eric Holder announced that Khadr would be tried by military commissions; not a regular court.

Edney and Whitling next approached the Federal Court seeking remedy for the fact that Khadr's rights had been violated. The Federal Court gave the Canadian government seven days to compile a list of possible remedies. The government launched an immediate appeal to the Federal Appeals Court. As far as the Harper government was concerned, there was no way Khadr was going to be compensated.

Meanwhile, in Guantánamo, the military commission hearing that Eric Holder had insisted on was in full swing. After initially pleading not guilty, Khadr was convinced by his US legal council to change his plea to guilty and agree that he would serve one year of a suggested eight-year sentence in a US prison. Doing so would make him eligible to be transferred to a Canadian prison to serve the remainder of the time.

Several months later, Khadr was still sitting in Guantánamo. He filed a clemency appeal to have his sentence cut in half. The appeal was denied. In August 2011, Khadr then fired his Edmonton-based legal team. Toronto-based lawyers John Norris and Brydie Bethell took up the cause.

Time dragged on. Finally in April 2012, US Defence Secretary Leon Panetta signed off on having Khadr moved out of Guantánamo. Khadr's Toronto legal team then filed a request to have him repatriated to Canada. This request became bogged down in legal wrangling. By early September 2012, Khadr was still in Guantánamo, his mental health starting to deteriorate.

His Toronto-based legal team obtained a report from psychiatric medical officials at Guantánamo. When this information landed in the hands of Canadian federal officials, things quickly start to happen. In late September 2012, Khadr was loaded on a plane and moved to Millhaven Penitentiary near Kingston, Ontario. In April 2013, Khadr again engaged his Edmonton legal team, this time to appeal his convictions in a US court. His lawyers argued that what he was convicted of doing was not a war crime under either American or international law. His legal team was successful in having him moved to a medium security facility in Innisfail, Alberta. The federal government immediately appealed the change of venue.

His appeal to the US court system to have his US convictions squashed was next denied. In May 2014, the widow of US Sgt. Christopher Speer along with the injured Sgt. Layne Morris filed a $134 million lawsuit against Omar Khadr. In 2015, a Utah court upheld the judgement. All they had to do now was collect.

In October 2014, his Edmonton legal team launched a $20 million lawsuit against the Canadian government arguing the government had collaborated with US officials to deprive him of his rights. Edney and Whitling also presented an argument that Khadr should be released on bail. In March 2015, the federal government argued that as long as charges were pending in the US, bail in Canada should be off the table. However, an Alberta judge decided to proceed with granting Omar Khadr bail. The federal government appealed the bail decision, but the Alberta Court of Appeals disagreed with the government's arguments and bail conditions were set.

In May 2015, Khadr was released from prison. Meanwhile, the $20 million lawsuit was working its way through the legal system. The politics in Ottawa also changed in late 2015. Stephen Harper was out as Prime Minister; Justin Trudeau was in. In July 2017, the federal government formally apologized to Khadr and agreed to pay him $10.5 million in compensation. In the spring of 2019, a judge ruled his eight-year sentence fully served.

Wow! What a difference Trudeau made. And I say that with sincere cynicism. Remember how Khadr's lawyers kept citing the 1982 constitution, arguing that his human rights were being violated? Should our government not have fought this to the bitter end? I have to wonder where this all would have ended up had Stephen Harper and the Conservatives stayed in power.

To top this saga off, in the winter of 2020, Omar Khadr was chosen to be the keynote speaker at Dalhousie University. He was invited to talk about child solder initiatives. What a joke! Thanks to the Trudeau Liberals, Omar Khadr was paid $10.5 million. Meanwhile, the death of US Sgt. Christopher Speer and the partial blinding of US Sgt. Layne Morris was ignored by the media. As for the Speer/Morris Utah lawsuit, in 2017 an

Ontario court ordered that the $10.5 million could not be accessed as part of settling the US lawsuit. Omar's father, Ahmed Said Khadr, who had the gall to send Omar and his two siblings to an al-Qaida training camp in Afghanistan, remains in the wind.

Dear reader, this whole saga can be summed up as follows: a father in Toronto sent his three Canadian sons to an al-Qaida terrorist training camp in Afghanistan. US Special forces invaded the camp. After the dust had settled, one of the US soldiers was dead and another was blinded in one eye. A youth in the camp (Omar Khadr from Canada) lay wounded. He was taken into custody and eventually moved to Guantánamo prison. Officials from Canadian spy agency CSIS were alerted that this Canadian youth was in captivity. The Canadian media found out about this situation. Two lawyers from Edmonton decided to get involved. After years of diplomatic wrangling, the lawyers were granted access to documents from Guantánamo. It turns out that young Omar had been interrogated and tortured. The lawyers launched a suit against the Canadian government arguing that Omar's constitutional rights had been violated. The Harper government fought hard against this lawsuit. In 2015, the Harper government was defeated and the Trudeau government was elected. Soon after, the government apologized to Khadr and offered him a settlement of $10.5 million.

So, how is it that a Canadian can join an al-Qaida terrorist group, be involved in the violence leading to the death of others, argue that his constitutional rights have been violated, and then get a cheque for $10.5 million?

What is going on?

CHAPTER 9

I do not always watch the television. I do not always turn on my cell phone. Sometimes I will go days without updating myself on news developments.

When I woke up on the morning of September 6, 2022, I turned on the television and discovered the province of Saskatchewan to be in shock.

On September 4, 2022, two men had gone on a stabbing spree on the James Smith Cree Nation (northwest of Melfort, Saskatchewan). At one point, they had even gone to the nearby town of Weldon, Saskatchewan. When this tragic spree ended, eleven people were dead and at least eighteen others were injured. The two men were actually brothers: Myles and Damien Sanderson.

I turned on my cell phone; it soon started blaring an alert. The amber alert warned that one of the two men was still on the loose. The alert was advising people to seek a safe, secure area at the sign of any danger. Law enforcement was unsure of where the second man had gone.

What's Going On?

It would soon be learned that the second man, Damien, had also been stabbed to death.

On Sunday evening, Canadian Prime Minister Justin Trudeau called the attacks "horrific and heartbreaking." If Canadians didn't have our ridiculousnessly restrictive gun laws, would the death toll have been this high?

A massive, province-wide manhunt finally brought the entire tragedy to an end on September 7. Police observed Myles Sanders in his vehicle traveling on a highway near Rosthern, Saskatchewan. When they forced the vehicle off the road, officers apprehended Sanderson. However, he was badly injured and died half-an-hour later while in police custody.

While the rest of the media was trying to close off on their dramatic reporting, an investigative journalist with Global News decided to break ranks with her colleagues and dig deeper into what had really happened. She discovered that the day before the rampage, Damien's wife, Skye, had called the Melfort, Saskatchewan RCMP detachment. She said that Damien had taken her car; he was driving around drunk, high on drugs, his brother in the passenger seat. The RCMP eventually located the abandoned car; returned it to her, and proceeded to do little else.

Further investigative probing by the journalist revealed that Myles Sanderson had amassed 59 criminal convictions by the time he was 31 years old. Damien Sanderson had two outstanding arrest warrants pertaining to assault incidents in 2021 and 2022. Further investigation revealed that Damien was actually afraid of Myles, who was unpredictable. It was further discovered, through discussions with Skye Sanderson, that Myles had been granted a statutory release in February 2022 after serving a four-year sentence for conviction on charges of assault, assault with a weapon, assaulting a police officer, uttering threats, mischief and robbery.

What is a statutory release you ask? Let me tell you what the Government of Canada says on the subject: *Historically, many offenders were granted early release based on a calculation of time off for good behaviour. In 1992, the* Corrections and Conditional Release Act (CCRA) *replaced this with statutory release. It is a type of conditional release because the offenders are supervised in the community. Unlike day and full parole, however, it is not granted by the Parole Board of Canada (PBC). Statutory release does not end an offender's sentence. Instead, offenders serve what is left of their sentence in the community. They must report regularly to a Correctional Service of Canada (CSC) Parole Officer and follow conditions. On statutory release, offenders have some time under supervision in the community before their sentence ends to help them return to society as law-abiding citizens. Offenders serving life sentences do not get statutory release. A statutory release in Canada is one where a person who has been serving prison time in a federal prison is given early release. The person is supposed to spend the remainder of their sentence under supervision of a parole officer.*

So, there you go. Rack up 59 criminal convictions. Go to a federal prison for a while. Get let out early and return to your community where you will be supervised. Truly unbelievable!

Myles would often telephone Damien from prison. Damien got tired of hearing from his brother and broke off contact. But contact was re-established in February 2022 when Myles was released from prison. Soon enough, Myles started coming to visit Damien and Skye at their house. He seemed to always have cocaine with him when he stopped by for a visit. Damien and Skye were both on prescription medication to help them deal with anxiety and depression. But crack cocaine was just too attractive and soon Damien started using. His behavior became dark and violent. Skye says she reported his behavior to the RCMP on several occasions, but nothing was done, no action was taken.

Skye said that one night when Myles was visiting, he suddenly started openly musing about killing his ex-common law spouse and maybe taking out 10 other people at the same time. In the end, it turned out that his musings of murder were more than just talk.

In my opinion, this tragedy highlights the failure of the Canadian corrections system. It highlights the reluctance of law enforcement to take action when residents call to express fear and concern. It highlights the failure of government—at the local band council level, the provincial level, and the federal level. The law enforcement system and the corrections system are failing people.

Is this the society that my grandsons have to look forward to? If one, or both, of the Sanderson brothers had banged on your door; drunk, stoned, flashing a knife, what would you have done? If you had a gun, would you have used it?

This all ties back to what I discussed earlier. We are not hard wired to be living the way we are. Now magnify that several times in the context of First Nations people. Crammed onto reserves, shacked up in substandard housing conditions. These are people who not so long ago were in step with Nature. These are people who have a deep reverence for Mother Earth. These are people who not so long ago were skilled at living off the land, hunting, fishing. We have stripped them of their identity. We have crushed their souls.

This gut-wrenching tragedy reflects on several themes discussed in earlier chapters: is the criminal justice system working? Would there have been as many deaths if those confronted by the killer were better armed? Could this situation have been stopped before it spiralled out of control?

CHAPTER 10

I am growing more and more worried about the increase in violence in society. Everywhere I look, I see violence. Video games are all about warfare and violence. Many movies on Netflix, Prime, and Crave streaming platforms have violence built in to their story lines. People are just exposed to violence way too much. Consider the following few incidents:

- On December 14, 2012, in Newtown, Connecticut, USA, 20-year-old Adam Lanza shot and killed 26 people. Twenty of the victims were children between six and seven years old, and the other six were adult staff members. His weapon of choice was an AR-15-style semi automatic rifle.
- On October 1, 2017, Stephen Paddock, a 64-year-old man from Mesquite, Nevada, opened fire on the crowd attending the Route 91 Harvest Country Music Festival on the Las Vegas Strip. From his 32nd-floor suites in the Mandalay Bay hotel, he fired more than 1,000 bullets, killing 60 people. His weapons included fourteen AR-15-style rifles (twelve of which

- had 100-round magazines), eight AR-10-style rifles, a bolt-action rifle, and a revolver.
- On February 14, 2018, 19-year-old Nikolas Cruz opened fire on students and staff at Marjory Stoneman Douglas High School in Parkland, Florida, 42 miles from Miami. He murdered 17 people and injured 17 others; his weapon of choice, an AR-15-style rifle with multiple clips.
- On May 24, 2022, a mass shooting occurred at Robb Elementary School in Uvalde, Texas, United States, when 18-year-old Salvador Ramos, a former student of the school, fatally shot nineteen students and two teachers, and wounded seventeen others. His weapon of choice, an AR-15-style rifle.
- On November 13, 2022, three University of Virginia students were killed and two were wounded when a gunman, a former football player, opened fire.
- On November 20, 2022, five people were killed and 17 injured when a gunman opened fire in a Colorado Springs, Colorado LGBTQ nightclub.
- On November 22, 2022 in Chesapeake, Virginia, a Walmart employee opened fire in an employee break room as the store was preparing to close for the night. Six co-workers were killed.

One common denominator to all these events was the use of an AR-15-style assault rifle. The other commonality is mental illness. Each of these people needed help. The health care system let them down.

Granted, these are American incidents. Yet, here in Canada, government figures show the proportion of homicides that involved a firearm rose from 26% of all homicides in 2013 to 37% in 2020. All it will take is for these assault type weapons to find their way into Canada and we will have a shit-show on our hands.

In May 2020, the Trudeau government took action when it announced a ban through Order-in-Council on more than 1,500 models and variants of assault-style firearms, such as the AR-15 and the Ruger Mini-14.

We certainly do not need AR-15-style assault rifles. I know people who own semi-automatic .22 calibre rifles, 4-shot semi-automatic shotguns, and .308 rifles. That's it. That's all a person needs, whether it be for hunting or for getting rid of gophers in the farm field.

The Trudeau government insists that it has no intention of pursuing other long-barrel guns such as hunting rifles and shot guns. However, as I noted earlier, mistrust of the federal government is growing. People I regularly speak with have a hunch that Mr. Trudeau has an agenda when it comes to guns. They feel there is another restrictive step coming in his gun policy.

I think the Saskatchewan government has similar suspicions about federal gun policy. On December 1, 2022 Premier Scott Moe tabled the *Saskatchewan Firearms Act to Protect Law-Abiding Firearms Owners*. Essentially this bit of legislation says, back off federal government, we here in Saskatchewan will take care of ourselves.

I grew up around guns. I sincerely hope that my grandsons grow up with a healthy respect for guns. I hope they learn how to use a gun in a sensible manner.

Do you know of someone who has been robbed? Have you ever been robbed? Even if it has never happened to you, it is something to think about? Do you have a home security system? Do you lock your house? Your car? Garage? Do you go outdoors at night and walk around the block? In an unfamiliar city, would you feel comfortable walking around freely?

Do you have insurance for your home to insure your valuables? How much does this cost you? Have you bought insurance to protect against vehicle theft?

The way I look at it from my 74-year-old viewpoint is that if a senior citizen runs into danger, we are at a significant disadvantage; we are the weaker and older. Thieves nowadays are much younger; they know that a senior is an easy target. We cannot protect ourselves. Hell, the law isn't even on our side. Consider the following scenario: You see someone

What's Going On?

in trouble, such as a neighbour being attacked. What do you do? What can you do? Most people would advise calling 911. The average time for 911 operators to pick up the phone is twenty seconds. Then you have to describe the situation to the 911 operator. Then you have to wait for the police to respond. Sorry, too little, too late.

If you have a gun, do you pull it out and go help your neighbour! Section 35 of the *Criminal Code of Canada* says that we have the right to defend ourselves using reasonable defensive actions. But using a gun to defend a neighbour? That is not in the cards, I am afraid.

Think about it. If someone is facing a serious situation and serious harm, all we can do is stand idly by after calling 911. Government statistics show that around 10% of seniors each year are victims of crime; mostly property crime. We cannot even pull a gun out and wave it at the thief. Does this sound right? No, not in my opinion. But then again, I am 74 years old, full of common sense, and very much aware of what it was like back in the good old days when common sense was the name of the game.

If a criminal breaks into a senior's home, what can a senior do? Run and hide? What if the criminal gets physically violent with the senior? When I was younger, getting bumped and bruised was no big deal; I healed quickly. But I am older now; things are a lot different. When a senior takes a beating, healing takes a lot longer. In many cases, the person never returns to normal.

You work hard for your entire career. You want to enjoy your senior years and suddenly some son-of-a-bitch wants to break into your house and steal from you.

Maybe a person should just have a gun. That would certainly deter any want-to-be thief. Call me radical.

I often get together with some of my senior friends for a cup of coffee. One morning in late 2022, we got to talking about crime and what is happening in our society today. An article in the newspaper showed that in 2021, Saskatchewan had 70 murders, 15 of them in Regina alone. Per capita, Saskatchewan has one of the highest murder rates in the country. Many of the murders were gang-related. Regina ranked #3 in Canada in the violent crime severity index. From 2020 to 2021, the violent crime severity index reading for Regina rose 16%. Regina Police Chief, Evan Bray, was quoted in the newspaper as saying, "We do know that gangs, drugs and firearms are all intertwined and so for us, it's not about just targeting one of those. We have real focused efforts on all three of those areas." Sure you do, Evan. Sure you do. Or is that just a politically correct statement for the media to lap up?

All very disheartening; for seniors and for my grandsons' futures. As I returned home that day after meeting my friends for coffee, all I could think about was the crime statistics. Where has society gone wrong? Where is society headed?

If you want to do an interesting exercise, do a Google search to find statistics pertaining to violence against seniors. The first two pages of links that the search will provide are all government statistics. Really? Are we to believe these numbers—or are the real numbers far worse? What do you think of the violence built into movies these days? Is it having a negative affect on our mental health? Was the federal government right in instituting a ban on assault-style weapons? Do you think people should have a gun in the house to act as a deterrent against break-ins? Much to consider.

CHAPTER 11

The subject of a citizen defending himself is a contentious one. Let's dig deeper.

I know a guy, Rodney, who owns a used car lot. The last time I ran into Rodney, he told me about an incident that happened a while ago. He had a problem at his car lot with thieves breaking into vehicles, stealing batteries, tires and anything they could get their hands on. I have known Rodney for many years. He is an ordinary citizen, trying to make a living running his used car lot. His car lot does not have an elaborate fence around it, nor is there an expensive security system. He could not afford any of that. Rodney is just an ordinary guy; a small entrepreneur trying to make a living doing something he enjoyed.

One of the vehicles on his lot is a used motorhome. Every now and again, Rodney and a buddy would sit in the motorhome after hours and have a few sociable shots of whisky. Rodney told me that one night, he and his buddy were sitting in the motorhome when they heard a voice outside; a group of thieves were checking out the motorhome, talking about breaking in. Except, the thieves were not aware that someone was inside the motorhome.

They waited quietly for the thieves to make their move. They heard the door being jimmied. They quietly retreated to the shadows at the back of the motorhome and waited for the thieves to enter. They gently shifted a curtain on a window to get a glimpse of what was going on outside. They saw three scraggly and scrawny thieves.

They heard one of them stepping on the stairs to get access to the door. It was time for two good old boys, both in shape, both strong, to teach these thieves a life lesson.

The question to ponder is, what would you do if you were Rodney? Would you take it upon yourself as a good, honest, hard-working person, to teach a group of useless scabs of society a life lesson?

The door swung open and one of the thieves entered the darkened motorhome. As he stopped to peer into the darkness, Rodney's buddy grabbed the wimpy, little thief and Rodney's fist made contact. Thud. A good hard punch caught the thief right in the mouth; down he went into a crumpled pile. Rodney and his buddy ran out of the motorhome to try to catch the other two thieves. No luck. They had heard the commotion inside and when they realized that the motorhome was occupied, they started running.

Back in the motorhome, the beating continued. When it was over, the unfortunate thief had a broken nose, a bleeding mouth and judging from his pain, a couple bruised or broken ribs. He was not going to go anywhere until the police arrived.

In a short time, two police officers arrived on scene and saw the predicament the thief was in. The police called an ambulance, and, in a few minutes, it arrived. The bruised and battered thief was hauled off to the hospital. The two police officers then said that excessive force had been used.

"Excessive force?" Rodney quizzed the officers. "What do you mean? They came onto private property, damaged the door on the motorhome and broke in. We were protecting ourselves." Rodney argued with the officers, explaining that they had been threatened, invaded, and now had a damaged door on the motorhome. The officers said that too much force had been used and they wrote him a ticket. Several weeks later, Rodney went to court to defend himself.

Rodney's legal counsel cited Section 34(1) of the Criminal Code while arguing that what Rodney had done to protect himself and his property was within bounds. With respect to defending yourself, Section 34(1) says: 34 (1) A person is *not guilty* of an offence if

>   (a) they believe that a threat of force is being made against them;
>   (b) the act that constitutes the offence is committed for the purpose of defending or protecting themselves;
>   (c) the act committed is reasonable in the circumstances.

Rodney's legal counsel then argued section 35 of the Criminal Code: A person is *not guilty* of an offence if:

>   (b) they believe on reasonable grounds that another person
>   (i) is about to enter, is entering or has entered the property without being entitled by law to do so,
>   (ii) is about to take the property, is doing so or has just done so, or
>   (iii) is about to damage or destroy the property, or make it inoperative, or is doing so;
>   (c) the act that constitutes the offence is committed for the purpose of
>
>   (i) preventing the other person from entering the property,
>   (ii) preventing the other person from taking, damaging or destroying the property,
>   (d) the act committed is reasonable in the circumstances.

The judge countered with Section 34 (2):

>   (b) whether there were other means available to respond to the

potential use of force;

(c) the person's role in the incident;

(d) whether any party to the incident used or threatened to use a weapon;

(e) the size, age, gender and physical capabilities of the parties to the incident;

(f) the nature, duration and history of any relationship between the parties to the incident, including any prior use or threat of force and the nature of that force or threat.

As far as the judge was concerned, this was a simple thief that had no prior association with Rodney. The judge said that Rodney was bigger and stronger than the thief. The judge said that Rodney had gone too far in doing what he did to the thief. The judge found Rodney guilty of assault. It was black and white, cut and dried. Case closed. Rodney now has a criminal record. He cannot travel to several countries, including the US, because of the criminal record.

Rodney's story raises an interesting issue. What if Rodney had been a senior citizen? What if he had used something like a stick to beat the thief? Would the judge have even stopped to consider the fact that there was a senior citizen involved? Or is being a senior citizen not a mitigating factor? The way I see it, we seniors, we baby boomers, need to start making noise. We need to start demanding that we should have the ability to defend ourselves. It will be a fight as we start to make noise, but we need to start making that noise right now!

Elie Wiesel, a Romanian-born American writer and Holocaust survivor said, "There are many times when we are powerless to prevent injustice, but there must never be a time when we fail to protest." And yes, it is time we seniors stand up! We need clarification on the term "reasonable force." If we stay quiet, the criminals will end up having more rights that the victims. This cannot be allowed to happen!

And while on the topic of what is reasonable—did you know that, according to the Criminal Code, it is illegal to carry a weapon for self-defence? A weapon can be anything designed or used or intended to cause death or injury or even just to threaten or intimidate another person. Let's say I had a pocketknife on my person. When I was growing up, a lot of us had pocketknives. They were useful for cutting a rope, cutting the twine on a bale of hay, and other odd jobs. If someone attacked me and I used my knife to protect myself, an officer of the law might charge me. Depending on how the judge saw the arguments, I might end up being charged with carrying a concealed weapon.

Let's say you are attacked and are capable of breaking free. You break free from the attacker and then decide to defend yourself. You beat the attacker (as in Rodney's situation) to the point where the attacker can't take another run at you. The judge could very easily determine that you did not have to beat up the attacker. You would then be found guilty of assault, just like Rodney.

What about using a firearm to scare off would-be intruders or someone whom you thought would do you harm? On a farm near Port Colborne, Ontario, a man named Ian Thompson was jolted out of bed at 6:30 a.m. by the sound of explosions outside of his secluded farmhouse. It turns out that Mr. Thompson had been having a disagreement with a nearby neighbour. The neighbour had been making unsubstantiated allegations that Mr. Thompson was a pedophile. The neighbour went so far as to pay a group of hooligans to throw Molotov cocktails at Thompson's house to set part of the house on fire. The neighbour figured that would be enough to scare Mr. Thompson and maybe he would move away from the area.

Here is where things got silly. It turns out Mr. Thompson was a former firearms instructor. As the Molotov cocktails were flying, he got his handgun, exited his house and fired three rounds into the air, which caused the assailants to flee. No people were hurt, although one of the owner's dogs was singed and there was about $10,000 damage to his home. A review of footage from Mr. Thompson's security camera showed one of the hooligans threatening to shoot him in the leg and then yelling, "Come here. I'll blow your f---ing brains out."

When the police arrived on scene, they arrested Thompson on charges of careless use of a firearm and unsafe storage of a firearm. They then seized his firearms and ammunition. The police then went so far as to pressure Mr. Thomson to enter a lesser plea and forfeit his right to ever own firearms again. Mr. Thompson refused and decided to fight the matter in court. The court ultimately found him innocent on all charges. The court battle took two-and-a-half years and over $60,000 in legal fees. The neighbour who had instigated the whole episode was sent to jail on charges of arson and endangering a human life. He served less than two years.

Commenting on his ordeal, Mr. Thompson said, "The Crown seemed to have an agenda to make an example of me and to put the fear into every firearms owner in Canada that you're not allowed to defend your life in circumstances like I faced."

We seniors, we boomers, should look at Mr. Thompson's case carefully. Was this right? Common sense is drifting away. Agendas are creeping in. Democracy is a fragile construct.

What do you think of the Thompson case? How do you think the law should address the situation of people defending themselves?

CHAPTER 12

I am getting tired of the confusion being sown by our elected officials in the House of Commons. Where is the common sense?

A good example is the controversial Bill C-11. In February 2022, the government tabled Bill C-11 (the *Online Streaming Act*). All the Conservative MPs voted against the Bill. The Liberals, NDP, Bloc Quebecois, and Green Party all voted in favor. C-11 purports to update Canada's 1991 Broadcasting Act and bring it into the modern, online era. The explosive issue surrounding this Bill is that it will define a "program" as any audio-visual content. Bill C-11 will give the Canadian Radio-television and Telecommunications Commission (CRTC) power to regulate the audio-visual content. The exact wording in the Bill references that online undertakings shall clearly promote and recommend Canadian programming, in both official languages as well as in Indigenous languages.

Bill C-11 has been poorly described and poorly explained. In my opinion, Bill C-11 is a confusing mess. In an earlier chapter, I mentioned that the venerable Henry Kissinger recently co-authored a book with Google pioneer Eric Schmidt. Their book stares down the entire artificial intelligence (AI) issue. The algorithms that run the big search engines and streaming platforms have taken on a life of their own. There are no human programmers overseeing these algorithms. To illustrate, go to YouTube and watch a video. The algorithms that run the YouTube platform know what you are watching. They will quickly start suggesting other videos of a similar genre that you should watch. Before long, all you will watch are videos of one viewpoint, one genre. This is how people and countries become politically and ideologically divided. The Kissinger/Schmidt book warns that due to these algorithms, society could be on the cusp of losing touch with reality.

The way I see it, Bill C-11 is the Canadian federal government (through the CRTC) trying to tell the big tech companies to reign in their algorithms and modify their source codes. Perhaps the Bill should have made this expressly clear. Instead, its confusing language has managed to stoke fear and mistrust towards the government. People think Bill C-11 is about government control of the people through control of the internet. Maybe our elected officials in Ottawa should be made to read the Kissinger/Schmidt book.

Regulate online content? As Kissinger and Schmidt make clear, the algorithms are a global phenomenon. There is no regulating to be done. YouTube cannot and will not create a special algorithm just for Canada. The CRTC can demand whatever it wants from the players who control the internet and social media. These players will just laugh at the CRTC.

Bill C-11 has now found its way through the Senate. As Canada's first Prime Minister, Sir John A. MacDonald, called it—the place of sober, second thought. Well, thankfully our Senators were sober and were capable of second thought when presented with Bill C-11.

Alberta Senator Scott Tannas summed it up nicely when he said, "There is no problem that the government can't make more complicated."

But not everyone in the Senate was thinking as clearly as Senator Tannas. During the Senate examination of C-11, Senator David Adams Richards, an acclaimed novelist, screenwriter and poet spoke at length. His comments were eloquent, riveting, and totally misguided. Here are some of the points from his February 3, 2023 speech:

The idea of any hierarchical politico deciding what a man or woman is allowed to write to fit a proscribed national agenda is a horrid thing. In Germany, it was called the National Ministry for Public Enlightenment, and every radio station was run by Joseph Goebbels—complete ideological manipulation in the name of national purity. No decree by the CRTC should tell us what Canadian content should or should not be.

I'm not speaking solely of the internet because I am too old to know it; however, this will bleed over into any performance we tend to create, and we will have government officials holding a book of rules telling us if we are Canadian enough or, worse, who can write what about whom.

By this Bill, we have entered the very realms we have fought to depose over the last 70 years. Bill C-11 might be more subtle than the German Stasi or the cultural section of the Central Committee of the former Soviet Union, but never think it is not intertwined.

As I write these comments in March 2023, Bill C-11 has received three readings in the Commons and in the Senate. It will soon be passed into law.

What is your opinion of the seeming inability of our politicians to clearly explain what a Bill is about?

Another Bill that is stoking controversy is Bill C-18, otherwise known as *The Online News* Act. As was the case with Bill C-11, this Bill is poorly worded. This Bill targets what it calls news intermediaries; the big internet platforms. Suppose a newspaper reporter in Saskatoon crafts a story and posts that story to his employer's website. Next, suppose the algorithm at a large internet platform picks up that story and re-posts it. Bill C-18 suggests that the large internet platform should pay money to the Saskatoon newspaper. Once again, our politicians do not grasp the power and reach of the AI algorithms. The Kissinger/Schmidt book should be mandatory reading.

In March 2023, a Parliamentary Committee summoned Sundar Pichai (CEO of Google and its parent company Alphabet), Kent Walker (President of Global Affairs and Chief Legal Officer at Alphabet) and Richard Gingras (Vice President of News at Google) to appear in Ottawa. Guess what? All three individuals snubbed the request and did not show up. These big operators are not willing to compensate smaller news outlets for news items. At this time of writing, Bill C-18 has received three readings in the House of Commons and is now being studied by the Senate.

There are rumored to be more Bills being drafted by bureaucratic strategists. These include C-26 (*Critical Cyber Systems Protection Act*) and C-27 (*Digital Charter Implementation Act 2022*).

What are your thoughts on the big platforms that run the internet? How does society prevent them from dominating what we see, hear, and read online?

I will conclude this chapter with some further frustration I have; this time with the Canadian Broadcasting Corporation (CBC). There is something like 6,200 full time CBC employees. Up until 2016, these employees each received a year-end bonus in the range of $1,300. In 2017, the bonus number jumped to near $2,100 per employee. In 2019, the bonus number was around $2,500 per employee. In my opinion, a largely government backed organization paying a bonus is fine so long as that bonus does not come from taxpayers. In late 2021, Prime Minister Trudeau asked Heritage Minister Pablo Rodriguez to steer the CBC away from generating advertising revenue. Trudeau told Rodriguez that this move would modernize the CBC. To compensate for the lack of ad revenue, Trudeau told Rodriguez that the government would provide CBC with an extra $100 million for each of 2022, 2023, 2024, and 2025.

I ask you—do you listen to or watch the CBC? Do these numbers change your desires?

All this spending raises another question. How deep in debt is Canada anyhow? Take a look at the website for the *Canadian Taxpayers Federation* (taxpayer.com). There is a link on the site to a website called debtclock.ca. This site shows a clock, which by the second, shows Canada's debt and its growth. As I write these comments on March 20, 2023, our debt is $1,212,056,201,000 trillion. Just to spell this out, that is one trillion, two hundred and twelve billion, fifty-six million, two-hundred and one thousand. There is plenty to go around. Every man, woman, and child in Canada has a $34,604 share. The growth of our debt (with interest) is close to $145 million per day. This means that every hour of every day, the deficit grows around $6 million dollars. I will repeat this—in Canada every day we wake up, we are around another $145 million dollars in debt.

CHAPTER 13

Another thing that keeps me awake at night is the thought of general government control of the citizenry.

In September 1959, Soviet Premier Nikita Khrushchev (in office from 1953 to 1964) spoke in Washington at the National Press Club. Prior to the visit he had gone on record as saying, "We will bury capitalism." To the journalists present at the Press Club event, he offered a reminder that his prior comment about burying capitalism not be taken literally. He said gravediggers carry a spade, dig graves, and bury the dead. What he had in mind with his statement was the outlook for the development of human society. He felt that communism will inevitably succeed capitalism. He reinforced his thoughts a few days later when he addressed the United Nations in New York. In that speech, he took a bolder stance, saying, "Your children's children will live under communism, You Americans are so gullible. No, you won't accept communism outright; but we will keep feeding you small doses of socialism until you will finally wake up and find you already have Communism. We will not have to fight you; we will so weaken your economy, until you will fall like overripe fruit into our hands. The democracy will cease to exist when you take away from those who are willing to work and give to those who would not."

Communism succeeding capitalism. Scary thought, in my opinion. No wonder I have trouble sleeping at night. The way I see it, communism is a scenario where the government has total control of the population. From what I have read, there are nine steps that lead to communism. All involve a weakening of the economy. Here is a list of the nine steps as I have come to understand them. As you read this list, think of what has happened over recent years, and what is happening today:

1) Health – get control of health care. Make sure the government will tell you what is good for you. In my opinion, this is what COVID has done. The government is now telling us what to do.
2) Poverty – make sure you have a large population base of people who are poor, as they are easy to control and will not fight back. Today the cost of everything is going up rapidly – food, gas and necessities. In my opinion, people today are getting poorer. Will we soon lose our will to fight back?
3) Debt – continue to encourage people to take on debt until it reaches an unsustainable level. Where are we headed today? Credit card debt is surging. As of late 2022, Equifax data shows Canadian auto loan delinquencies to be climbing aggressively. In Q3 2022, about 1.97% of auto loans had become delinquent. Equifax data shows the rate hasn't been this high in at least a decade. Add to this the fact that interest rates are rising. The cost of carrying debt is starting to hurt.
4) Control Guns – make sure people will not have any individual power to protect themselves. This is already happening. Take a look around.
5) Welfare – have as many people as possible on welfare so they have food, housing, income, so they fall under full government control. Government control grows as more and more people are in this situation.
6) Education – ensure government control over what the education

system is telling young people what is best for them.
7) Religion – take it out of schools and eliminate any possibility of children having religious beliefs.
8) Class Welfare – slowly shrink the middle class and have a large number of people who are poor as they are much easier to control.
9) Media – control the media. The CBC in Canada is under total control of the government. A hard turn has now been made to steer away from generating advertising revenue. The government will fully fund the CBC with taxpayer money. Whatever amount of money they need, the present government gives them. Are they going to be critical of what is happening? Would they ever criticize this government? Would they bring out facts that the government might not approve of? Of course not! Bill C-11 and Bill C-18 represent further efforts at government control of the media.

Let's take a quick look at what is happening today and tie it in to the slow creep towards the decay of a country. As I was contemplating writing this book during COVID, one day I took some time to flip through the *Regina Leader Post*. The date of the paper was July 5, 2020. Here are some of the headlines:

Page 1 – Province to fund up to two hundred new addiction spaces
Page 2 – Medicines fought 60 years ago the same symptoms similar to COVID-19
Page 3 – Sask Gaming posts $19.1 million dollar profit after the reopening of casinos
Page 4 – $2.1 million dollars pledged to fund first year (this had to do with addictions)
Page 5 – Pupils from Ukraine quickly adjusting
Page 6 – (half a page of a weather map, and the second half is a government ad connecting with Canadians about their health)
Page 7 – (cartoon depicting the passport problem)

Page 8 – (cartoons and word games)
Page 9 – Love Conquers Clutter
Page 10 – (top half of the page) TV Times Tonight
Page 11 – New regs will boost gas price. (This story caught my attention. Here is a quotation from the article: *With Canadian gas prices continuing to hit historic heights, the Trudeau government has quietly rolled out a latticework of new fuel standards that are expected to permanently raise gas prices by an amount equivalent to the federal carbon tax. The new clean fuel regulation, unveiled last week, would force energy companies to reduce the "carbon intensity" of gasoline and diesel.*

Well, isn't this something! Earlier in this book, I made the argument that we have seen a migration away from the rural and towards larger population centers. We no longer walk out the back door to the garden. Now we have to drive to a grocery store. We no longer walk across the yard to start our chores in the barn. Now we drive to a job. A job that many of us hate, working for bosses many of us loathe. It makes us unstable. We have come to rely on a vehicle to get around. Now gasoline prices are going to keep rising, year after year. What happens to those people with lesser incomes? Simple—they get poorer, the middle class shrinks and socialism stirs on the horizon.

In 1982 with our Constitution repatriated, Canada began a slow ebb towards being more forgiving. Interpretive legal challenges to the Constitution Act have given criminals more rights. The Criminal Code has been revised and the thought of protecting yourself became questionable. Reasonable and unreasonable force came under scrutiny. Criminals who break into your home can claim you used unreasonable force. You, the homeowner, could be charged. The examples in recent chapters illustrate this.

I came across a fascinating article from Global News in January 2023. Journalists Elizabeth McSheffrey and Emad Agahi described how a civilian group in Dawson, British Columbia started patrolling the streets. These citizens call themselves *Citizens Take Action*. Dawson Creek is a small town, population about 12,000. As Doug Scott, the leader of the group points out, "You have an individual who commits a property crime—he steals whatever he can find—the RCMP finds the guy, arrests him, and he's back on the streets 10 minutes later. Our town runs around scared. Twenty people keep doing 80 percent of the crime." Doug Scott explains that his group conducts regular patrols through the town. He acknowledges that confrontations do happen, but his members try to avoid confrontation. He admits his group is operating in "the grey zone and riding the line." For the record, RCMP Staff Sgt. Kris Clark said, "The RCMP cannot condone or support vigilantism." Meanwhile, British Columbia Attorney General Niki Sharma is assuring residents that the province's *Safer Communities Action Plan* will result in improvements to the Dawson Creek situation. Peace River South MLA Mike Bernier calls it as he sees it. He claims, "Somebody is going to get hurt in all of this. Things will escalate."

The interesting thing about this article is that it got no traction from other media outlets. Of course not! The federal government does not want the rest of the country knowing that a town in British Columbia is conducting its own citizen patrols. I suggest that when you come across articles like this one, print them off, clip them out, save them. When someone suggests to you that everything is rosy, peachy, and wonderful in society you will have material to present an argument with. The more people that become aware of what is really happening in the country, the better.

This example from Dawson, BC is a reminder that we can get organized. We can stand up for ourselves. What are your thoughts?

CHAPTER 14

Let's look a bit deeper at the subject of controlling health care—one of the steps in creating country decay and leaning towards communism. The way the COVID pandemic was handled will be debated, discussed, and argued over for years to come. The lockdowns, the vaccine mandates—all of it is seared into our memories. The whole thing was mishandled. Not just in Canada; in the US too. Was this by accident or was this by design?

The World Health Organization (the WHO) was a key player in the COVID pandemic. Where did the WHO come from? The answer—it was created by the United Nations in April 1948. The events leading up to the creation of the WHO are something that more people should be aware of.

The early 1800s marked a wholesale change in human interaction. People were coming to major European centres in search of jobs. With the masses came disease; in particular cholera. As industry flourished, more people came. As more people came, cities and towns became severely crowded. Filth and disease flourished.

Governments did not sit idly by. Sanitary Conferences were convened to discuss how to reduce disease. Medical Congresses were convened to standardize medical treatment procedures. But it was not all smooth sailing. Some governments started to push back, refusing to accept the policies and procedures advanced at these conferences and congresses. Finally in 1907, a general consensus was reached. Belgium, Brazil, Egypt, France, Great Britain, Italy, Netherlands, Portugal, Russia, Spain, Switzerland, and the United States of America all agreed to create a new body, the Office International d'Hygiene Publique (OIHP). Delegates to its meetings would be technically trained individuals. In 1920, the OIHP was made a permanent part of the League of Nations. Progress was made over the next 20 years, but political unease between nations acted as a damper on the speed of progress. The war years placed a severe strain on the ability to meet and on the ability to conduct research and develop policies. In 1944, the OIHP was folded into a new body, the United Nations Relief and Rehabilitation Administration (UNRRA). What is not commonly known is that in 1902, the US government established a regional health body called the Pan American Sanitary Bureau (PASB). This bureau gave its full cooperation to the OIHP. But in 1913, that all changed when a new group inserted itself into the PASB equation: the Rockefeller Foundation. Under guidance from the Rockefeller Foundation, the PASB quickly grew and in 1948 became the framework for the WHO.

The Constitution of the WHO lists 22 separate functions that the WHO is mandated to undertake. The first of these is broad in its sweep; to act as the directing and co-ordinating authority on international health work. Another function is to stimulate and advance work to eradicate epidemic, endemic and other diseases.

There are three parts to the WHO. The first part (or *organ* as it is called) is the World Health Assembly. Each country sends three delegates to the Assembly meetings. Each delegate has one vote. The Assembly approves a general programme of work and gives instructions or directives to the Executive Board and the Director General. The President and officers are elected at each Assembly meeting. The Assembly has the power to adopt policies and regulations concerning sanitary and quarantine requirements and other procedures designed to prevent the international spread of disease.

The second organ is the Executive Board. The Constitution gives the Board the power to submit proposals and advice to the Assembly, prepare general programmes of work for approval by the Assembly, and to take, or authorize any action required in an emergency, for example, an epidemic or a calamity. In total, there are 34 members on the Board. The Board has the authority to take emergency measures within the functions and financial resources of the WHO to deal with events requiring immediate action. In particular, it may authorize the Director General to take the necessary steps to combat epidemics.

The third organ is the Secretariat. The Secretariat is divided into three major departments: the Department of Technical Services (Division of Epidemiology, Division of Editorial and Reference Services, and sections of Health Statistics and Therapeutic Substances), the Department of Operations (Planning and Field Operations), and the Department of Administration and Finance.

Article 2 of the Constitution of the World Health Organization prescribes that in order to achieve its objective the Organization shall establish and maintain effective collaboration with the United Nations, specialized agencies, governmental health administrations, professional groups and any other appropriate organizations, and promote co-operation among scientific and professional groups which contribute to the advancement of health.

Article 66 says: The Organization shall enjoy in the territory of each Member such legal capacity as may be necessary for the fulfilment of its objective and for the exercise of its functions. Article 67 says: The Organization shall enjoy in the territory of each Member such privileges and immunities as may be necessary for the fulfilment of its objective and for the exercise of its functions. Article 72 says: Subject to the approval by a two-thirds vote of the Health Assembly, the Organization may take over from any other international organization or agency whose purpose and activities lie within the field of competence of the Organization.

The bottom line is, the WHO is one mega-powerful body. The following questions all become very valid once the power and reach of the WHO is realized: Was COVID developed in the Wuhan, China lab? Why are we vaccinating children when the number of children getting sick is a small number? Were Pfizer and Moderna actually paying governments for the number of vaccines being administered?

With regards to the lab in Wuhan, China, I encourage readers to study the report by Congressman Michael T. McCaul. Your eyes will be opened—wide.

What are your thoughts on COVID? Was this a virus designed to gather data on how the population would respond to it, how the population would react to mask mandates, vaccine mandates, travel restrictions, and mRNA vaccine efficacy?

CHAPTER 15

What is or who is the Rockefeller Foundation? On the surface, it advances the new frontiers of science, data, policy, and innovation to solve global challenges related to health, food, power, and economic mobility.

Behind the scenes, the Rockefeller Foundation has not limited its influence to just the WHO. The primary goal for the Rockefellers has always been globalization, where a group of corporations and organizations control the global economy. In the 1950s, the advanced countries had 22% of the global population and controlled 62% of global GDP. In the 1960s, the Rockefellers became worried that this level of dominance had hit a plateau and that globalization might falter. They, along with a tight-knit group of like-minded people decided that they needed to take a direct role in promoting globalization. To create a formal platform to promote globalization, David Rockefeller created the Trilateral Commission.

An acquaintance of the Rockefellers, Swiss Klaus Schwab believed that the management of a modern enterprise must push to extend the boundaries of globalization and in 1971, he founded the European Management Forum. He promoted the "stakeholder" management approach, which based corporate success on managers taking into account of all interests: not merely shareholders, clients and customers, but employees and the communities within which they operate, including government.

These two business clubs soon attracted political and corporate elite members. Meetings turned into ripe opportunities for new policies, programs, and partnerships. Events in 1973, namely the collapse of the Bretton Woods fixed exchange rate mechanism and the Arab-Israeli war, saw the European Management Forum expand its focus from management to economic and social issues. In January 1974, political leaders were invited for the first time to the annual Davos meeting. Two years later, the organization introduced a system of membership for the "1,000 leading companies of the world." As a show of its influence, the European Management Forum was the first non-governmental institution to initiate a partnership with China's economic development commissions, spurring economic reform policies in China.

In 1987, the European Management Forum became the World Economic Forum and sought to broaden its vision to include providing a platform for political dialogue. *The Davos Declaration* signed in 1988 by Greece and Turkey saw them turn back from the brink of war. In 1989, North and South Korea held their first ministerial-level meetings in Davos. At the same meeting, East German Prime Minister Hans Modrow and German Chancellor Helmut Kohl discussed German reunification. In 1992, South African President de Klerk met Nelson Mandela and Chief Mangosuthu Buthelezi to discuss the country's political transition. Schwab's Forum was now without doubt a significant influencer of corporations and nations alike.

A visit to the World Economic Forum website reveals some interesting information. For example:

- COVID-19 likely originated in wild animals sold in open food markets. The virus easily jumped to humans because farmers had cleared and settled large areas of natural habitat, increasing interactions of wildlife with people, including as food. Sanitary standards at markets were poorly regulated, while rapid transport between densely populated cities spread the virus globally. Now whether infected people become seriously ill or die depends on their underlying health and nutrition, as well as their access to healthcare, sanitation and adequate housing. Indeed, COVID-19 is a story of multiple systems impacting each other, triggering a host of unintended consequences impossible to understand, let alone manage, without looking at them together.

- In the ongoing COVID-19 pandemic, real-time data about travel patterns that spread disease has been very difficult to quantify. With an exponential rise in mobility and growing global connectivity, this data will be critical to planning surveillance and containment strategies.
- Instead of handing out money for recovery bailouts, we should seek to transform the economy with public funds that push companies to improve working conditions, reduce carbon emissions, and reverse the excessive use of share buybacks.
- How farmers produce food determines not only the fertility of their soils, but the health of the planet. The food systems of tomorrow must embrace the One Health vision and advance positive interactions between human health, livestock health, wildlife health and ecosystem health. This approach can minimize the spread of disease, ensure adequate water for crop irrigation, reduce destructive flooding and wildfires, and protect farmlands from intense climate events, while also sustaining forest, grassland and wetland habitats. Farmers should be helped to diversify their incomes and incentivized to farm productively. Sustainable food systems must be central to strategies.

Wow! Read this stuff again. The Forum is telling you with certainty where COVID came from. Whether infected people become seriously ill or die will depend on their underlying health and nutrition. So, who determines a person's underlying health and nutrition? The world needs more technology for surveillance and containment. In other words, people on the planet will be watched as to their every move. Farmers will diversify their incomes and become environmental stewards. The next eight or so years will be about ecosystem restoration.

One issue that has been causing farmers to get upset is talk by government that fertilizer application rates must be reduced. Many farmers have pointed a finger at Prime Minister Trudeau. In theory, he is not the architect of any sort of plan to reduce fertilizer application rates. The creators of that plan are way above his pay grade. He, his Ministers, and their bureaucrats are all just doing what they are told. Did you know that Canada's very own Chrystia Freeland is on the World Economic Forum Board of Trustees? In my opinion, this is placing Canada's toes a little too close to the fire. Here is what alarms me. It has been suggested to me that in the next election if voters replace Mr. Trudeau with a Prime Minister that wears a different colored uniform, nothing will change. The Rockefellers and the Davos crowd are just too powerful. A country that fails to listen will be brought to its knees, quickly. A politician that fails to listen will be disposed of in short order. I hope this is not the case—but if it is, then we are doomed, to be blunt about it.

Where is this all taking us? Schwab makes this very clear on the World Economic Forum website. He asks, "What kind of capitalism do we want?" He goes on to explain, that if we want to sustain our economic system for future generations, we have three models to choose from. The first is "shareholder capitalism," embraced by most western corporations, which holds that a corporation's primary goal should be to maximize its profits. The second model is "state capitalism," which entrusts the government with setting the direction of the economy and has risen to prominence in many emerging markets, not least China. The third model is "Stakeholder capitalism," which positions private corporations as trustees of society, and is clearly the best response to today's social and environmental challenges. What he is really alluding to is that government will no longer be in charge. Corporations will call the shots and run the world. Those corporations will be subservient to Davos, and likely also to the Trilateral Commission.

In 2020, the World Economic Forum released a new *Davos Manifesto*. This platform makes clear that: *companies should pay their fair share of taxes, show zero tolerance for corruption, uphold human rights throughout their global supply chains, and advocate for a competitive level playing field.*

In order to implement stakeholder capitalism, companies will need new metrics. Schwab says that: *a new metric of "shared value creation" should include "environmental, social, and governance" (ESG) goals as a complement to standard financial metrics. Fortunately, an initiative to develop a new standard along these lines is already under way, with support from the "Big Four" accounting firms and led by the chairman of the International Business Council, Bank of America CEO Brian Moynihan.* He is indeed correct. Take a look at the financial statements of any oil and gas company or any mining company. An entire section of the financial statements and management discussion now is devoted to ESG. Can a company opt not to pursue ESG? Sure, they can, but they will be crushed by the tentacles of the Davos crowd. Pension plans will refuse to own shares in non-ESG-compliant companies. Auditors will refuse to perform annual audits. A company that refuses to adhere to ESG principles will be driven out of business, and quickly so. Shwab also says: *the second metric that needs to be adjusted is executive remuneration. Since the 1970s, executive pay has skyrocketed, mostly to "align" management decision-making with shareholder interests. In the new stakeholder paradigm, salaries should instead align with the new measure of long-term shared value creation.* What he is saying is that executives are going to start earning less money, and corporations will become subservient.

If one explores the Forum website in more detail, the reach of the Forum becomes downright scary. We are going to see full scale implementation of Facial Recognition Technology. Law enforcement organizations around the globe currently have this technology, but it is subject to error. The accuracy of the technology will be improved in the coming years. We will be watched in all that we do. Manufacturing is going to be reconfigured to include Artificial Intelligence (AI). The question to be asked is: where will humans fit in to the manufacturing process? Cities will be reconfigured and repurposed into "smart cities." Waste management, solar power, reduced manual labour, and automation will all come into focus in the coming years.

Will we all have a say in any of this? The answer is, "No." Is this what a majority of Canadians want? I sincerely hope that my grandsons grow up with a solid grip on technology. I hope that they are able to learn about AI and automation. I do not wish for my grandsons to be technology followers. I wish for both of them to be technology leaders.

Before we close this chapter, I would like to mention another shadowy group with their fingerprints all over the levers of global control. The group, actually the family, I speak of is the Rothschilds. The Rothschilds (German for *red shield*) are a European banking dynasty that traces their origin to the activities of Mayer Amschel Rothschild in 1774. Mayer's parents were Ashkenazi Jewish. After their untimely and early deaths, Mayer got a job apprenticing to a German banker. Following his apprenticeship, Mayer married and before long was the father of five sons.

The next several decades saw the family become skilled at trading coins and debt instruments; all typical stuff for a banker. The big tipping point for the family enterprise came with the French Revolution and the Napoleonic Wars. Mayer and his sons figured out how to work both sides of the fence. No matter who won a conflict, Mayer and his sons would benefit. They soon came to dominate trade throughout Europe in wheat, cotton, weapons, money transfers, insurance, and stocks. The British Industrial Revolution saw the family finance coal mining, railways, and manufacturing. Today, the descendants of the family are found in major global financial centers. They maintain a low profile, always staying true to Mayer's original philosophy: cooperate with one another and never aim for excessive profits. But, rest assured, their hands are firmly gripped on the levers of global political and financial power.

CHAPTER 16

In a previous chapter I made the radical comment that maybe we seniors need to get a handgun to provide a deterrent against crime. Let's look at that statement more closely, as radical as it might be.

Want to buy a handgun in Canada? Forget it. Not going to happen. In October 2022, Prime Minister, Justin Trudeau announced a national freeze on the sale, purchase, and transfer of handguns. Yep! A freeze! From now on people cannot buy, sell, or transfer handguns within Canada, and they cannot bring newly acquired handguns into the country.

Offering some wisdom on the decision he said, "Canadians have the right to feel safe in their homes, in their schools, and in their places of worship. With handgun violence increasing across Canada, it is our duty to take urgent action to remove these deadly weapons from our communities. Today, we're keeping more guns out of our communities, and keeping our kids safe."

Bill C-21 relied on data from a Statistics Canada study published in 2020. The study looked at two periods: 2009 through 2014, and 2015 through 2020. The study used police-reported incidents of firearm related crime: homicide, physical assault, robbery, uttering threats, and violent offenses. The study defined violent offenses as: discharging a firearm with intent, pointing a firearm, or use of a firearm in the commission of an indictable offence.

The way I see it, this study was a difficult one. Canada is a geographically diverse country. Within the geographic diversity is economic diversity. Ignoring these layers of diversity and just looking at gun incidents as a measurable statistic is potentially fraught with error.

This Statistics Canada report states that in these two reporting periods, 59% of police-reported gun offenses involved a handgun. My question is, if over a 12-year period there has been no increase in handgun offenses, what then is the basis for Bill C-21?

The report shows that homicides were just under 2 per 100,000 of population in 2009 and at 2 per 100,000 in 2020. Not a statistical difference, the way I see it.

Physical assaults involving a gun were 7 per 100,000 population in 2009 and 8 per 100,000 in 2020. Not a significant statistical difference, the way I see it.

Robberies involving a gun were 14 per 100,000 population in 2009 and 8 per 100,000 in 2020. That is a notable *decrease*, the way I see it.

Uttering threats while using a gun were 2 per 100,000 population in 2009 and 3 per 100,000 in 2020. Not a significant statistical difference, the way I see it.

Violent offenses (discharging a firearm with intent, pointing a firearm, or use of a firearm in the commission of an indictable offence) were at 2 per 100,000 population in 2009 and at 6 per 100,000 in 2020.

Statistics can also be potentially misleading. A move from 2 to 6 over a 12-year period is a tripling of occurrences. Or, one could say that the *geometric growth rate* in this statistic is 12.5% per year. One could also say that the *arithmetic growth rate* is 33% per year. Take your pick. What sort of conclusion do you want to arrive at? But of course, no politician is going to start citing *geometric* and *arithmetic growth rates* because people don't understand this sort of mathematics. Call it a failure in our education system, call it a failure in our ability to critically think, call it what you wish. Statistics can be used to whitewash any study involving data and we don't question the data.

The way I see it, the government used a single study and focused only on violent offenses. At a rate of 6 per 100,000 population (that is 0.006%), Bill C-21 was quickly crafted and made into law. This is a government that does not want the citizenry protecting itself.

The subject of weapons is complex, but really boils down to a series of definitions: *non-restricted, restricted, and prohibited.*

A non-restricted weapon includes ordinary hunting and sporting rifles, shotguns and airguns with an overall length of 660 mm or greater. Many airguns fall into this class because they are capable of achieving a muzzle velocity of 500 feet per second. This definition includes centrefire semi-automatic firearms providing the barrel length is greater than 470mm (18.5 inches). Want to buy a non-restricted shotgun or a rifle for hunting? That is still possible. In Canada, people 18 and over who want to buy a non-restricted long gun must take the *Canadian Firearms Safety Course*, and then get a *Possession and Acquisition Licence* (PAL). A pair of exams is required along the way. One exam is written, the other practical. You will need a grade of 80% or more to pass each one. Then the police will do a criminal check on you, which will take some time. The fee associated with that is $80. Then there is a 28-day waiting period. To store a non-restricted weapon, you must do it in one of two ways: unloaded with a trigger or cable lock in a locked box, or unloaded in a safe.

Here is the problem, the way I see it. With all these measures in place, you cannot quickly use your stored, locked-up gun to protect yourself. If you do not have it securely stored and can access it to get off a warning shot, you can find yourself fighting the same court battle that Mr. Thompson fought in Port Colborne, Ontario. Even if you did have quick access to the weapon, you could still be potentially charged for unreasonable use of force.

What is a *restricted weapon*? Section 84 of the Criminal Code contains the definitions you need to know. A restricted weapon is a weapon that has a barrel less than 470 mm in length (18.5 inches). If it is capable of discharging centre-fire ammunition in a semi-automatic manner, then it is restricted. It is also restricted if it is designed or adapted to be fired when reduced to a length of less than 660 mm (26 inches) by folding or telescoping. Restricted weapons also include many handguns. Or, at least that is how it was up until October 2022.

What if you already own a restricted gun? Be careful, for Section 95 of the Criminal Code says a person is guilty of an offence if they are in possession of a restricted gun (loaded or not) while not having a license or a registration certificate. Make damn sure you get your *Possession and Acquisition Licence*. Section 96 of the Criminal Code forbids you to be in possession of a restricted gun that was previously used in committing a crime. So, don't even think about buying a gun on the street from a shady character who might have committed a crime with it. Section 100 of the *Criminal Code of Canada* says if you are not licensed to possess a restricted or even a non-restricted firearm, then don't even think about trying to transport the weapon. Know someone in the US who can sneak a gun into Canada for you? Think again. Section 103 of the Criminal Code says that by importing you are guilty of an offense. The maximum penalty for violating sections 95, 96, 100 or 103 is now 14 years behind bars as per Bill C-21 passed in 2022.

What is a prohibited weapon? Again, section 84 has the definitions. Prohibited weapons include all fully automatic firearms and converted automatics. All variants of the AR-15 genre of rifle are prohibited. A prohibited firearm is a handgun with a barrel less than 105 mm in length (4-1/8 inches). This pretty much covers all handguns. To make sure nothing is missed, the definition also includes handguns capable of discharging .25 or .32 calibre bullets. People are allowed to use handguns (if they already own one) in sporting competitions governed by the rules of the International Shooting Union, such as the Shooting Federation of Canada.

A prohibited firearm also includes sawed-off shotguns. The definitions say that if a person saws off a shotgun so that the total length of the modified gun is less than 660 mm in length (26 inches), then that weapon is prohibited. What if a person saws it off so that the length is just over the 660 mm length? Authorities will measure just the length of the barrel. If it is less than 457 mm in length (18 inches), the weapon is prohibited.

Boomers are aging and many live in fear of being robbed or assaulted. We want to be able to protect ourselves in the event our home is broken into. Here is a simple, common-sense question: if you are in your dwelling with a gun with which to protect yourself, will you use the gun to hurt anyone? It's not like you are going to use the gun to rob the 7-11 store down the street from your house. All you want is some manner of protection within the four walls of your home. I am pretty sure the vast number of seniors reading this book will agree. Yet, common sense no longer applies. The government will not allow us to have a gun in our home for protection.

I will wrap this chapter with a real example from 2010. Perhaps if the people in this story had been in possession of a gun, they would be alive today. The story involves two seniors, Lyle and Marie McCann, who were just shy of their 58th wedding anniversary. They were taking a road trip, travelling in their motorhome from Alberta to Chilliwack, BC. Their burned-out motorhome was discovered at an Alberta campground and the vehicle they were towing was found thirty km away. To this day, their bodies have never been found. A local 38-year-old-man, Travis Vader, described by law officials as a desperate drug addict, was charged with their deaths. In September 2016, an Alberta court convicted him of two counts of second-degree murder.

Here is where I have to question the intelligence of the judiciary. Vader's clever lawyer argued that the judge had failed to look at the most up-to-date version of the Criminal Code, which of course ties in elegantly with the *Charter of Rights and Freedoms*. Vader's lawyer applied to the Court to have his client's sentence reduced to manslaughter. Instead, the Court decided to sentence Vader to a single charge of murder with no chance of parole for seven years. With some good behaviour behind bars, Vader will soon be out and free. Yes, indeed. What if, just what if these two seniors had been in possession of a gun?

CHAPTER 17

I have done a lot of reading lately about how criminals are getting treated by our legal system. On one hand, I am dismayed. On the other hand, downright afraid of what is happening.

What many people reading this book may not fully understand is that in 1982 when our Constitution was repatriated, the government of Pierre Trudeau added a section to the Constitution called the *Charter of Rights and Freedoms*. It is a lengthy read, but I encourage everyone to find the document online and read it. Better yet, read it with your grandchildren. Somehow, I doubt this stuff even gets talked about in the school system anymore.

The Charter in a nutshell says: Everyone has the following fundamental freedoms:

(a) freedom of conscience and religion;

(b) freedom of thought, belief, opinion and expression, including freedom of the press and other media of communication;

(c) freedom of peaceful assembly; and

(d) freedom of association.

What's Going On?

Let's talk about a crime in the context of this Charter. To be found guilty of a crime, a person must exhibit a guilty action (*actus reas*) and have a guilty mind (*mens rea*). The guilty act must be voluntary.

The Charter of Rights and Freedoms has become a tool for clever lawyers to use when defending clients. In my opinion, this is just plain wrong. Consider this twisted bit of legal thinking: a lawyer could argue that if a person voluntarily consumes intoxicating drugs or alcohol, it is a violation of the *Charter of Rights and Freedoms* to say that the intoxicated person then voluntarily committed a crime. But, the Criminal Code of Canada says otherwise. It says in Section 33(1): A person who, by reason of self-induced extreme intoxication, lacks the general intent or voluntariness ordinarily required to commit an offence nonetheless commits the offence if

(a) all the other elements of the offence are present; and

(b) before they were in a state of extreme intoxication, they departed markedly from the standard of care expected of a reasonable person in the circumstances with respect to the consumption of intoxicating substances.

In other words, a person who becomes intoxicated and commits a crime is still guilty of the crime. So, which document is correct? The Criminal Code or the Charter? A 2019 case in Saskatchewan peeled back the layers of the onion, so to speak.

In Regina, Saskatchewan in January 2019, Blake Schreiner murdered his wife, Tammy Brown. Police found her body in the couple's home. She had been stabbed 80 times. Schreiner's clever lawyer made it clear in court that, yes, his client had killed his wife. Yet, his lawyer argued that the murder charges should be *reduced* to that of manslaughter. His lawyer explained that his client had used magic mushrooms (psilocybin), along with alcohol. These substances had put him into a blackout state. Thus, he was unable to form the necessary guilty mind (*mens rea*) to commit murder. Where the case got even more complicated was Schreiner had kept a series of personal, written journals. He had documented in his writings how he had been using magic mushrooms, even on the evening of the murder.

When Mr. Schreiner gave his testimony, he admitted that he and his wife had been drinking together. He described how he experienced a blackout which was interspersed with brief hallucination-like memories in which he saw himself stabbing his wife repeatedly. His lawyer said those hallucinations and the amnesia accompanying them show the man was not in a state of mind to be able to form the requisite intent to commit murder. A court-appointed pharmacology expert described for the court how Schreiner would not have been in a state of mind to commit murder. In the end, the judge convicted Schreiner of second-degree murder and sentenced him to 17 years without parole. As far as I am concerned, this should have been first degree murder; locked up for life with zero chance of parole. Yet, a clever lawyer playing on the Charter managed to get the conviction reduced.

A similar case occurred in 2018. In this case, the accused had no pre-existing mental issues. On the night of January 12, 2018, Matthew Winston Brown was at a party in Calgary, Alberta. He consumed alcohol and hallucinogenic magic mushrooms. Brown left the party and broke into a nearby home and violently attacked a woman, Janet Hamnett, with a broom handle. Ms. Hamnett suffered permanent injuries to her arms and hands.

Mr. Brown was charged with aggravated assault, breaking and entering, and mischief to property. He had no previous criminal record and no history of mental illness. Thanks to clever lawyers steering the case through appellate courts, the matter eventually made it to Canada's highest court.

Writing for a unanimous Supreme Court, Justice Nicholas Kasirer said section 33(1) of the Criminal Code violates sections 7 and 11(d) of the Charter in a way that cannot be justified in a free and democratic society and is unconstitutional. He wrote that section 33(1) violates section 11(d) of the Charter because society could interpret someone's intent to become intoxicated as an intention to commit a violent offence. Section 33(1) also violates section 7 of the Charter because a person could be convicted without the prosecution having to prove that the action was voluntary or that the person intended to commit the offence. In other words, a guilty

What's Going On?

action (*actus reas*) and a guilty mind (*mens rea*) are not present when a person is intoxicated to the point of grossly impaired consciousness. The winner here is Matthew Winston Brown, the loser is Janet Hamnett.

Here is the problem, as I see it. These nine judges live in a different world than most Canadians. The chief justice makes $403,800 and the other eight members make $373,900. These people can afford elaborate homes with hi-tech anti theft alarm systems and surveillance systems. The vast majority of Canadians do not have these luxuries. These judges have no idea what it is like to live on month-to-month pension checks or social assistance checks. Some seniors even end up getting a part time job to support themselves financially. The Supreme Court of Canada has told not only seniors and women, but all hard-working people, that if a drunk or meth-head decides to attack you in your home, beat up your kids, rape your wife, or steal your possessions, the criminal has a defence in the form of grossly impaired consciousness. Have you heard the media warning about this? I surely have not.

Holy crap! What is going on? Where is all this headed? A reduced conviction in a Saskatchewan case. A unanimous Supreme Court ruling on an Alberta case. And now, here we go with another layer of confusion! On January 31, 2023, British Columbia became the first jurisdiction in the country to start what will be a three-year experiment on drug decriminalization. Drug users aged 18 and over will be allowed to carry a combined 2.5 grams of opioids like heroin and fentanyl, as well as cocaine, methamphetamine and MDMA (ecstasy). Watch what happens as these people start committing violent crimes. The Supreme Court has already ruled on the issue of crime committed when a person is intoxicated to the point of grossly impaired consciousness. Maybe my earlier comment about seniors having a gun readily available in the confines of their residence is not so radical after all.

Have you heard the media taking an issue with all this? I surely have heard very little. All I have heard is CBC blathering on about the three-year trial decriminalization period in British Columbia. No effort has been made to connect the dots and warn people of the possible consequences.

That's not what the Trudeau government wants us to hear. Can you believe all of this? We are losing our country. It is time to wake up.

Let's go one step further and look at sexual offences. In my opinion, the Trudeau government and the judiciary in Canada want to roll back the Harper-era tough sentence requirements for sexual offenses. The term that I hear being used is *proportionate sentencing*. Consider the 2022 Supreme Court case involving Eugene Ndhlovu. He had been charged with two counts of sexual assault, tried, and sentenced to six months in prison plus three years probation. His name was added to the sex offender registry (SOIRA). There were also a number of other reporting requirements: providing extensive personal information, updating information in person yearly, reporting any changes in primary or secondary address, reporting receipt of a driver's licence or passport, and notifying authorities of intention to be away from his primary or secondary residence for seven or more consecutive days. Ndhlovu found a clever lawyer and took the matter to the Supreme Court. He argued that these restrictions breached Section 7 of the Charter. The Court ruled the restrictions to be "overbroad." Here we go again. A sexual offender being given more wiggle room thanks to a clever lawyer, a sympathetic judiciary, and the Charter.

In 2008, former Nipawin, Saskatchewan school teacher Jeremy Houston was convicted of being in possession of child pornography. He applied to the appellate court and decided to defend himself. He argued that the images found in his possession in 2005 "were stamped with URLs of legitimate adult websites, each having disclaimers that the models depicted are over 18 years of age." In addition, he argued, "One image of a 17-year-old girl showed the upper cleavage of her breast only, with no nipple exposed." The judge bought Houston's arguments. Jeremy Houston received an 18-month conditional sentence followed by three years of probation. During both terms, he is confined to his home except for medical emergencies, religious purposes, or with the consent of a supervisor, and he is also banned from using a computer or the Internet.

Here is a hypothetical situation. I am beyond certain that one day very soon, a situation like this will occur in a town or city near you. Gina, a Grade 12 high school student, is at home one afternoon studying for exams. She has been harassed by a 19-year-old boy named Butch. She had first met Butch at high school. They dated on two occasions; once to a movie and once out for dinner. There was no sex involved and she politely told him she was not interested in seeing him anymore. He kept wanting to see her, and she kept nicely telling him via phone and text message that she was not interested in seeing him. As she sat at home studying, there was a knock on the door. It was Butch. He said he had a present for her. She opened the door and he barged in. She asked, "You said you had something for me?" He then said "Ya, sex." He grabbed her, she started screaming and he punched her in the mouth to shut her up. He punched her several more times, ripped the clothes off her and repeatedly raped her. As she lay on the floor bleeding from her mouth, he gave her two kicks to her head, leaving her unconscious. A half-hour later, she regained consciousness, found her cell phone and called her mother who immediately called the police, the ambulance, and her father. When her parents arrived, Gina was in a terrible condition. The police and ambulance arrived moments later. Gina mustered enough energy to say it was Butch, whom the parents had met. After the ambulance left, Gina's dad said, "I am going to kill that bastard." He was mad and sad as to what happened to his daughter. The police knew of Butch and promised to find him and bring him to justice. The police delivered on their promise, finding Butch and charging him with rape and bodily assault.

Standing before the judge, clever lawyer at his side, Butch explained he had been high on crystal meth and alcohol. Butch's clever lawyer cited the Supreme Court decision of May 2022 and the issue of grossly impaired consciousness. The lawyer argued that Butch's actions were not voluntary because of the alcohol and drug intoxication. The judge had no recourse but to find Butch not guilty.

Is this what Canadians want? In my opinion, we are losing our country. And we are not even aware of what is happening because the media is not beating the drum loud enough. Arguments built around the Charter are giving criminally-active people more wiggle room to do what they want. I repeat—senior citizens are at risk. We are at increased risk of being robbed, beaten, and shot. We lack the ability to physically fight back against an assailant. We will be targeted more often. Assailants getting caught will then be represented by clever lawyers seeking to strut their legal acumen and Charter arguments in front of higher courts. "Oh, your Honour, my client had a bad upbringing. He took to drugs as a coping mechanism. At the time of the alleged offence, he was suffering from grossly impaired consciousness." The sympathetic judge will then put the accused into a taxpayer-funded program to help with rehabilitation. And what about the person who got badly beat up? This is quite the democracy we have. Or should I say, we *had* a democracy.

And the slow erosion continues. In May 2022, the Supreme Court unanimously ruled that life sentences without the chance of parole are both cruel and unconstitutional. The ruling went on to say that sentencing mass killers, including terrorists, to whole-life sentences is as cruel as whipping them would be. Whole-life sentences are therefore unlawful under the Charter of Rights and Freedoms. The ruling further added that sentencing killers to lengthy prison terms with little hope of freedom risked bringing the administration of justice into disrepute. Life without hope of parole shakes the very foundations of Canadian criminal law, deprives individuals of autonomy and is incompatible with human dignity. Acknowledging the heinous crimes of those serving multiple life sentences, Chief Justice Richard Wagner wrote that the ruling must not be seen as devaluing the life of innocent victims.

Can you believe this? Have you heard about this in the media? Not likely. Yet, it is happening. And here is the stinging insult. The ruling is retroactive to 2011. I wonder how the families of people who were murdered by these criminals feel.

Let's look at some examples:

- In 2017, Alexander Bissonnette killed six Muslims at a mosque in Quebec City. He was handed a 40-year sentence. He will not have to serve the whole sentence.
- In 2014, 24-four-year-old Justin Bourque of New Brunswick killed three Mounties. His sentence says no parole eligibility

until the age of 99. I doubt he will serve time until the age of 99.
- In 2015, 24-four-year-old Derek Saretzky of Alberta murdered a two-year-old girl and two adults. He was handed a life sentence with no parole eligibility for 75 years. I doubt he will be sitting in a cell that long, thanks to the Supreme Court.
- In 2014, Douglas Garland of Alberta killed three people when he was 57. He was sentenced to life with no parole eligibility for 75 years.
- In 2018, Alek Minassian of Toronto killed ten people and injured many others when he veered his van into a crowded sidewalk. He was sentenced to life with no parole eligibility for 25 years. Will he serve the full 25 years?

Is this what Canadians want? As far as I am concerned, the Supreme Court ruling is a joke! Our nine, highly paid, judges in their fur-trimmed robes are out of touch with reality.

The issue of bail reform also rips me up. On March 29, 2018, the Government introduced Bill C-75 to amend both the Criminal Code, the *Youth Criminal Justice Act* and other Acts. The bill was passed into law on June 21, 2019.

The Charter of Rights and Freedoms (Section 11b) says that people have a right to be tried in a reasonable time. Bill C-75 was designed to ensure that accused people would have a limited stay in detainment prior to a court hearing their case. Bill C-75 recognized that strict bail conditions or less than pleasant conditions in remand centers would have negative repercussions on a person's health and well-being, family and social relationships, and livelihood. Bill C-75 was also designed to expedite the movement of cases through the legal system to free up court time.

The Bill removed the use of preliminary hearings. Generally speaking, preliminary inquiries are used to test the strength of the Crown's case prior to proceeding to trial. Adults charged with an indictable offence under the Criminal Code will normally have the right to seek a preliminary inquiry, should they wish to. Bill C-75 restricts preliminary inquiries to only the most serious of offences.

The Bill removed the ability for lawyers to refuse to accept a potential juror for no well-stated reason. This is called a "peremptory challenge." One of the ways that Bill C-75 seeks to foster diversity is through the creation of a more equitable juries.

The Bill orders that courts exercise restraint when imposing bail conditions. The Bill also tackled AOJO's (Administration of Justice Offenses). For example, suppose a person was charged with a crime and released on bail. Suppose that person then committed another crime; but one where nobody was physically hurt. Bill C-75 says the presiding judge can ignore the new crime, adjust the terms of bail, or revoke bail. It all comes down to improving Court efficiency. Police officers are busy. What if an arresting officer is unable to attend a court hearing for an accused person? The entire case could end up being thrown out of Court. Bill C-75 allows for an officer to submit written statements to the Court without having to physically attend. Again, improved efficiency.

Bill C-75 reared its ugly head in late 2022. Rookie OPP officer Constable Grzegorz Pierzchala was called to assist with a car in the ditch near Hagersville, Ontario. When he arrived at the vehicle, he was gunned down by the occupants: Randall McKenzie, 25, from the Mississaugas of the New Credit First Nation and Brandi Stewart-Sperry, 30, from Hamilton. In 2018, a Court had told McKenzie he was prohibited for life from possessing any firearm. But, in 2021 McKenzie was charged with several firearm-related offences as well as assaulting a peace officer. He was released on bail, charged with weapons offenses. Bail conditions included remaining in his residence and not possessing any firearms. He was supposed to answer to the charges in September 2022, but he failed to attend court. A warrant was then issued for his arrest. McKenzie and his partner have now been charged with first-degree murder in the shooting death of Const. Grzegorz "Greg" Pierzchala.

OPP Commissioner Thomas Carrique said of the matter, "The murder of Constable Greg was preventable. This should have never happened. Something needs to change. Our police officers, your police officers, my police officers, the public deserve to be safeguarded against violent offenders who are charged with firearms-related offences. I'm outraged by the fact that McKenzie was out on bail and was provided the opportunity to take the life of an innocent officer."

The Conservative Party is now demanding that the Trudeau Liberals repeal some parts of Bill C-75, especially when it comes to firearms offenses. A motion put forth by the Conservatives was handily defeated by the Liberal minority with help from the Bloc and the NDP. In light of the tragedy in Hagersville, Ontario, I have to ask—where is the common sense in the House of Commons? I encourage you to speak with your member of Parliament. Ask that person—what is going on?

CHAPTER 18

2022 was a year to remember. In late 2021, Russian leader Vladimir Putin decided he wanted to take back the eastern part of Ukraine. He started to mass troops and military vehicles along the border as the world looked the other way. In February 2022, the troops advanced. Ukraine was under siege. Why?

In 1979, the Soviet Union staged an invasion of Afghanistan. This decision would prove to be the economic ruination of the Soviet Union. The financially costly conflict dragged on for 10 long years. The Soviet leader responsible for spearheading the Afghan conflict was Leonid Brezhnev. When he died in 1982, he was succeeded by former KGB boss Yuri Andropov. But Andropov only remained in power for two years, dying in 1984. He was succeeded by Konstantin Chernenko, who only ruled for one year before dying. In 1985, Mikhail Gorbachev assumed the levers of power.

Gorbachev was not the usual Soviet leader. He had an inclination for a more peaceful world. He could see that the Afghan conflict had ruined his country. He reached out to US President Ronald Reagan. Gorbachev pulled his military out of Afghanistan. He withdrew troops from central and eastern Europe as well. He was instrumental in scaling back the scope of Soviet nuclear weapons. He played a key role in having the Berlin Wall torn down. The world was now a better place. But all the change had opened the door for domestic upheaval.

In 1990, a hard-line group of men who wanted Moscow to retain its communist ideology started to gain in popularity. But Gorbachev ignored them. He proceeded with further reforms. He orchestrated the unification of East Germany and West Germany. This drew severe criticism from the hardliners. In August 1990, Iraqi leader Saddam Hussein invaded Kuwait. Gorbachev signalled his support for US military action. This further angered the hardliners. By late summer of 1991, Gorbachev had lost his ability to influence politics in Moscow. The hardliners had become too popular. A major blow to the Russian economy was delivered on December 1, 1991 when Ukraine held a referendum and overwhelmingly opted for independence. Ukraine had been an economic engine for the Soviet Union: wheat, sunflower oil, sugar beets, cattle, coal, oil, and natural gas.

As Ukraine embarked on its path of independence, political economist and former chairman of the Soviet Ukraine Republic, Leonid Kravchuk, stepped into the position of President of Ukraine. In 1994, Kravchuk lost his bid for re-election to Leonid Kuchma. However, the going was far from smooth for Kuchma. It soon came to light that he had deep ties to a group of Russian oligarchs. To deflect criticism and to get the media to look the other way, he fired his entire Cabinet along with his Prime Minister Viktor Yushchenko. He replaced Viktor Yushchenko with Anatolii Kinakh. A year later he fired Kinakh and replaced him with Donetsk regional governor Viktor Yanukovych.

In 2004, Ukraine decided to have its first democratic elections as an independent state. By this time, things had gotten ugly for Kuchma. The people took to the streets, staging protests, strikes, demonstrations, and concerts that will be remembered in the history books as the Ukrainian Orange Revolution. One of the revolution organizers was political activist Yulia Tymoshenko.

Kuchma quickly slithered away, leaving the country. The final vote for the position of President came down to two candidates: pro-Russian candidate Viktor Yanukovich and pro-Western former prime minister, Viktor Yushchenko. In the end, Yushchenko prevailed with 52% of the votes. One of the campaign promises he had made was that, if elected, he would make Yulia Tymoshenko his Prime Minister. She was appointed and served in the role in 2004-2005 and again from 2007-2010. Under her leadership, significant economic reforms were implemented that drew Ukraine into closer alignment with the West. These reforms included a Membership Action Plan with NATO in 2008. Unfortunately, this Action Plan went nowhere. German Chancellor Angela Merkel and French President Sarkozy both got cold feet and reasoned that if Germany pressed ahead with welcoming Ukraine into NATO, Mr. Putin would retaliate by shuttering the flow of natural gas to Germany; France in turn would also suffer. This decision will be debated by geopolitical scholars for years to come. This decision may well have been a serious tipping point in world affairs. This decision may have been the one that gave Mr. Putin his "mo-jo" to double down on efforts to restore Russia to its former glory.

The next scheduled election in 2010 would prove controversial. Tymoshenko ran against Yanukovich. In the end, he won by a slim margin. To neutralize any chances that Tymoshenko would threaten his government, Yanukovich orchestrated criminal charges against her which saw her spend three years in prison. She was released from jail after the European Court of Human Rights got involved. She ran for office again in 2014 and 2019, losing out on both occasions.

Meanwhile, in 2013, Yanukovich formally rejected overtures from the United Nations to establish a more solid relationship with the West. Instead, he leaned towards Moscow and Vladimir Putin. He also opted not to make further progress on the issue of joining NATO, despite Ukraine having signed the 2008 Membership Action Plan. The failure of Yanukovich to move the country forward was too much. The Ukrainian people erupted in protest. The violence that followed is documented in the history books as the *Euromaidan*. Violence escalated to the point that by March 2014, Ukraine was in danger of backsliding into civil war.

Yanukovich resigned and fled the country, taking exile in Russia with his friend Putin. The parliament ordered new elections for May 2014.

Vladimir Putin was closely watching the events unfold. He was now in danger of losing his grip on politics in Ukraine. To stomp his foot down and assert authority, in March 2014, Putin staged an invasion and annexed the Crimean region of the country. This move effectively removed the people of the Crimean region from the voting register in the coming May elections. Putin then made sure his annexation efforts spilled over into the eastern part of Ukraine. He wanted to take back the Donetsk and Luhansk areas (collectively called the Donbas region). In April 2014, armed pro-Russian separatists made bold moves and declared the Donetsk People's Republic (DPR) and Luhansk People's Republic (LPR) as independent states. The big question that remains is why did Ukrainian troops not try to stop Putin's annexation efforts? It seems that Putin had done his homework. He had assembled a collection of senior military leaders all of whom had old loyalties to Moscow. His annexation efforts amounted to pushing on a door that was already half opened.

When the May 2014 electoral votes were counted, politician and businessman Petro Poroshenko emerged as President. He immediately got to work advancing the economy of Ukraine. His efforts resulted in an *EU-Ukraine Association Agreement*. The agreement committed Ukraine to implementing economic, judicial and financial reforms designed to bring it closer into alignment with the European Union. The European Union in turn agreed to provide Ukraine with political and financial support, access to research and knowledge, and preferential access to European markets. The actions of Russia also rekindled talk of joining NATO. Yet, Poroshenko failed to follow through. He wanted to remain militarily independent. Poroshenko then took action on the military front. He ordered troops into the Donetsk and Luhansk areas to push back Russian separatists. This miliary effort would drag on for the next eight years with thousand of casualties on both sides. In fact, the reported total casualty count is near 14,000 people. The rising casualty numbers would prove to be Poroshenko's undoing in the 2019 elections.

The 2019 election saw Poroshenko up against Volodymyr Zelensky, lawyer and television show production company owner. Zelensky campaigned on ending the conflict in the eastern part of the country. Zelensky's message resonated with the people and he won by a landslide.

Since the early 2022 moves by Putin, Zelensky has been making it very clear that Ukraine wants to join NATO. But easier said than done now. Being admitted to NATO would require a confirming vote by all the 30 member states. Joining NATO would effectively commit the other NATO members to enter Ukraine to fight against the Russian invasion. These other members are just not prepared to go that far. As an alternative means of supporting Ukraine, countries from around the world (Canada included) have placed sanctions on Russia, frozen oligarch bank accounts, and seized oligarch assets. Russia pushed back with threats of turning off the Nord Stream pipeline that flows natural gas into Europe.

In April 2022, the G20 Finance Ministers met in Washington. The Russian Finance Minister was streamed in virtually. When he attempted to interject on a point being discussed, Canadian Finance Minister Chrystia Freeland, Bank of Canada Governor Tiff Macklem, Chair of the US Federal Reserve Jay Powell, Ukrainian Finance Minister Serhiy Marchenko, and European Commissioner for Economy Paolo Gentiloni all got up and left the room in a display of anger towards Russia. But this cold-shouldered display would soon turn silly.

Not long after, Russia abruptly announced that its state-owned gas operator, Gazprom, would be shutting down a portion of the Nord Stream natural gas pipeline for regular scheduled maintenance. This had the potential to disrupt natural gas inventories in Europe. Gazprom had a standing contract with German turbine maker Siemens GmbH for repairs to the pipeline pumping station turbines. Canada then found itself in a tight squeeze. Siemens realized that it had a turbine engine sitting at its Montreal manufacturing facility. A desperate Germany approached Canada for help. Germany argued that Canada should exempt the turbine from sanctions and send it to Russia. This would speed up the routine maintenance activities the Russians were planning. This would ensure that Germany would not have to draw down its natural gas inventories as it waited for the Russians to complete the maintenance. Canada agreed to the German request. Volodymyr Zelensky was livid. How could Canada de-facto offer support to Russia when thousands of people had been injured and killed by the Russian invasion of Ukraine?

No doubt Mr. Putin was carefully watching the turbine drama play out. He likely concluded that the Trudeau government was weak. Mr. Trudeau defended the decision saying, "While it was a very difficult decision, Russia is trying to weaponize energy as a way of creating division amongst the allies. Canada's move was made to help Germany in the short term as it and other European countries work to reduce their reliance on Russian oil and gas. We took this difficult decision to be there for our allies, to ensure that in Europe, not just governments but populations stay steadfast and generous in their support of Ukraine."

Volodymyr Zelensky blasted Trudeau saying, "If a terrorist state can squeeze out such an exception to sanctions, what exceptions will it want tomorrow or the day after tomorrow?"

This question is very dangerous.

But then, Putin got a surprise shock. In fact, everyone got a shock. In late September 2022, an unknown, yet well-trained operative dove to the bottom of the sea and planted detonation charges on the Nord Stream pipeline structure. On September 22, the charges were set off. The pipeline ruptured and is now not fixable. Russia does not have the technical wherewithal to carry out the repairs. Any nation that has the ability is also levying sanctions on Russia, so the political optics are blurry.

We will never know who the operative was who planted the explosions, but it all conjures up images of something the US Navy Seals would get involved with. This explosion has played right into the hands of the United States. The US immediately responded to European concerns about not having enough gas to survive the winter. Tankers of liquefied natural gas (LNG) soon set sail from Louisiana bound for Europe. By late 2022, the US was sending 10 million cubic maters every month to Europe (the equivalent of about 63,000 barrels of oil per month). The Middle eastern nation of Qatar is sending the equivalent of 8.5 million barrels of oil per month to Europe. These US and Qatari figures will no doubt increase in subsequent years. The European economy is now badly wounded. The cost of bringing in natural gas by LNG tanker is far from cheap. Any competitive advantages European manufacturers had, are now gone, perhaps never to return.

Canada is sitting on a huge reserve of natural gas. At current consumption levels, Canada has 200 years of recoverable natural gas. Can Canada get involved in exporting LNG to Europe? Yes, we can. All we have to do is set up an LNG loading facility in a place like New Brunswick or Nova Scotia. Tankers can pull in, load up, and set sail for Europe. But there is one problem. That problem is Quebec. In 1971, Quebec started construction of the James Bay hydro-electric project. Today, that project generates approximately 83 Terawatts of power each year. That is enough power to supply two cities the size of Toronto with electrical power. The Quebec government is making serious profits selling this power to neighbouring provinces and US states. The Quebec government wants nothing to do with natural gas which could potentially fuel a generating plant and compete with the hydro from James Bay. To illustrate further, consider that TC Energy operates a large diameter natural gas pipeline that extends from Alberta to the Ontario-Quebec border. Yes, this pipeline stops at the Quebec border. Why? As I say, there is no way that the Quebec government wants natural gas flowing through its province. Electricity from James Bay will never see any competing sources such as natural gas fired generating plants. Case closed, end of argument. So, Canada loses out on lucrative LNG sales to Europe all because of Quebec.

This TC Energy pipeline is *not* operating at capacity; the pipeline is capable of flowing 7 billion cubic feet per day. As of late 2022, Canadian government figures show that the pipeline is moving just under 4 billion cubic feet per day. The reason for this lack of capacity utilization is the fact that the US is sitting on a sizeable amount of natural gas in New York and Pennsylvania. The gas is found in the Marcellus Shale formation. It is estimated that this geological structure can supply gas to eastern North American markets for 92 years. It is cheaper for end users in Ontario and the Maritimes to buy the US natural gas. Add to this the fact that in the Maritimes, the amount of available off-shore natural gas declined to being non-viable in 2018. Since then, natural gas has been imported from the US via the M&NP Pipeline which enters Canada at St. Stephen, New Brunswick. Wonderful. The Maritimes is importing US natural gas because Quebec will not allow a pipeline through their province.

People who are frustrated at the lack of movement of natural gas from the west to the east are quick to blame Trudeau. The reality is, Quebec politics rules the day. When Mr. Trudeau's government is eventually replaced by another political party, nothing will change on the movement of gas from west to east. The political party that assumes power after the Trudeau Liberals are gone needs the Quebec vote if it is to win subsequent elections. In fact, eastern Canada will likely never see an LNG facility exporting natural gas to Europe. The one remote possibility is a talked-about project in Newfoundland that will access gas from a geological formation called the Jeanne D'arc Basin. But that is billions of dollars in investment capital and years away.

Meanwhile, on the west coast, the situation is different. There are hundreds of kilometers of pipeline projects that are federal government approved; all designed to move natural gas to the Kitimat, BC area where an LNG plant is being built. This LNG will be exported to Asian markets, namely China, Japan, and India. These nations are taking aggressive steps to ramp up their LNG regasification infrastructure. So, here in the west, we don't need Quebec after all. I just feel bad for the people in the Maritimes who have to import US natural gas.

In June 2022, the G7 leaders met in Krun, Germany. The western media focused on the policy discussions. But a Chinese journalist took notes on what else was happening. He observed that as British Prime Minister Boris Johnson and Mr. Trudeau were sitting down for talks with US President Joe Biden and the rest of the G7 leaders, Prime Minister Johnson piped up and asked whether the Western leaders should "take our clothes off?" Johnson then quipped, "We have to show that we're tougher than Putin." This was a clear reference to the fact that Mr. Putin is in good physique and has been photographed shirtless on many occasions. Mr. Trudeau then chimed in suggesting that the group take part in a "bare-chested horseback riding display." Johnson replied, "We've got to show them our pecs."

And we voted these clowns into office? Actually, Johnson is no longer around. His decision to host an unmasked garden party at 10 Downing Street during the depths of COVID has since cost him his job. As for Mr. Trudeau, it is up to you. Vote in the next election. The decision is yours as to which party governs us.

So, the conflict in Ukraine drags on. The European economy is suffering. Canada is unable to export natural gas to assist. Our leaders openly talk about showing Putin their pecs when they meet for a G7 event. The western media ignores this banter, but a Chinese journalist writes about it. How embarrassing.

As of March 23rd, 2023, over 8,000 citizens have been killed and over 14,000 have been injured since the beginning of the Ukraine invasion in February 2022. Approximately 70,000 Russian troops have also been killed. The US government estimates the total of wounded and killed on both sides to be nearer to 200,000. One day, long after this book has been published, the real numbers will be revealed—and they will be staggering.

I will wrap this chapter with a question for you to ponder: What is this war all about? There are many theories floating around. Certainly, it is about Mr. Putin trying to restore Russia to her former glory. But there could be a darker side to it. American geopolitical author Peter Zeihan feels that America and the NATO countries deliberately did nothing as Putin was massing his troops on the eastern edge of Ukraine in late 2021. They wanted him to invade. Zeihan's theory is that the US and NATO are going to grind Russia down, perhaps drag the conflict out for years, with the ultimate goal to once and for all economically destroy Russia so that it never again poses a threat to any country, anywhere. NATO will feed Ukraine just enough weaponry to keep the conflict going. Ukrainians that die in battle will be collateral damage.

As of March 2023, tanks were arriving on the battlefield. In fact, NATO has provided $80 billion in weaponry to Ukraine since the start of the conflict. Ukrainian soldiers are now returning from training missions in various NATO countries; fully trained in how to use the latest advanced weapons systems sent to Ukraine. The soon-to-start spring offensive will be messy. Casualty counts will escalate.

Let me repeat myself. The world is witnessing a tragedy in Ukraine that seems to trace back to the 2008 decision by Angela Merkel and French President Sarkozy to deny Ukraine's entry into NATO. If Ukraine were a NATO country today, none of this conflict would be happening. The bigger question is, was this Merkel's and Sarkozy's decision alone, or did someone from the US State Department whisper some instructions in their ears? As early as 2008, was the US strategizing for a future battle in Ukraine?

CHAPTER 19

Every few days I get together with a small group of guys in Moose Jaw for coffee. Our coffee group is a mixed one. We have a couple retired farmers, a few business owners, a couple retired teachers, several retired union guys from the local phone and power utility companies, and some retired construction workers. The average age of our group is somewhere in the mid-70s. A few members of the group are relatively healthy with no major issues. Some have heart problems. Some have gone through knee and or hip replacements, some walk with canes, most have eyeglasses, a couple have hearing aids, a few have fought cancer and won, a couple were presently fighting cancer. Our group had lost a few guys over the years to strokes, cancer, and heart attacks. I imagine our group is typical of other coffee groups of 70-year-olds across the country. We sometimes call ourselves the Boomers.

One day after I arrived back home from having coffee with the Boomers, I sat down in my Lazy-Boy chair and started to relax. The sun was flooding in through the window. I started to feel sleepy; very sleepy.

Maybe it was that second doughnut that I had devoured? Maybe it was the chocolate chip cookie with a bit of cannabis in it?

My thoughts began to drift. I had visions of a group of us getting together for coffee. We were talking about the crime statistics. I drifted deeper into relaxation. Soon I was asleep. I began to dream. I was in the coffee shop …

CHAPTER 20

Brian had not shown up at the coffee shop that morning. One of the guys in our group said he heard that Brian's house had been broken into last night. He heard Brian was in hospital and he was hoping to visit Brian later that afternoon.

The next morning, we all got together again at the coffee shop. We learned that Brian's house had a good alarm system, but the intruders were able to bypass it. The three intruders hit, kicked, and punched Brian and his wife Beth. The intruders were not interested in large objects such as computers or the large screen TV. They wanted jewellery, watches, and rings. They even took Brian and Beth's rings off their fingers. As Brian and Beth lay on the floor, hurt and bruised, the intruders went through every room. They scooped up jewellery, ornaments, wallets, cash, and credit cards. We learned that both Brian and Beth were in the hospital. The doctor figured they would be in hospital for three, maybe four days. Brian and Beth's kids lived hours away. Their daughter was driving the six hours to get to her parents' house; their son was flying home today. As we sat around the coffee shop table dumbfounded at the news, one of our group said, "This is enough. That could have been any one of us. We need to do something."

What? Who said that? It was KC. He was a different sort of guy, hair flying all over place, kind of always messed up; a hippy throwback, a computer techie. He always wore weird, wire rim glasses; they just screamed computer genius. He was not much of a talker. Maybe genius types are not talkers?

He had told us on a few occasions that he had created apps for his smart phone. None of us were smart enough to know how phone apps were designed, so we usually just nodded our heads in approval. Sure, we all had smart phones, but designing apps was way over our heads.

Today he spoke up and actually began to string together sentences. We all looked at him in amazement. We had never heard this many words coming from his mouth. As he spoke, we all started listening; carefully. He said our smart phones could save us, keep us informed and keep us together. The actual expression he used was our phones "could keep us entangled."

We knew KC's wife had passed away three years ago. Now he told us that he was 76 years old and had one daughter who lived across the country that he saw about three times a year. He went on to say he was bored, had lots of money, and had been working on an app that was unique to anything we had ever seen.

He said the app could tie us all together, so if anyone had a problem of any kind, all they had to do was tap on the app icon on their smart phone's screen, touch the red button that appeared on the screen, and within seconds all the other app users would know the caller's exact location, right down to the street and house number. He explained the app could be installed on the touch screen display in a vehicle, on a desk top computer monitor, a tablet, a TV screen, and on any smart phone. He said it could even be installed on a wrist watch, or for that matter any wearable device that emitted a signal and that was connected to the Internet. He explained that the app was not all of his work alone. Over the past few years, he had been collaborating with a group of other app developers from around North America. Together, they had created the app. KC explained that this app was at least five, maybe ten years ahead of anything even remotely close to it. He said thanks to this app, we were now less than three seconds from letting everyone know if we were in trouble. All any of us could say was "WOW!" There was one more detail he added. He said he and his app develop friends had decided to call the app, "Boomware."

Over the next few days, 23 of us met with KC one-on-one. We would hand him our phones and a few taps later, his "Boomware" was installed in our phones. We did test runs and it was a lot of fun. It was absolutely foolproof. A few of our group drove miles out of town in various directions. They opened the app on their phones, hit the red button, and presto! All of our phones responded with a text message telling us where they were: grid road, and even farmyard location. Other members of our group drove around the city, stopped—hit the button and our phone screens all told us where they were. It all worked like a charm. If someone's vehicle stopped, we would get an alert showing us the exact spot. If someone's vehicle was moving, a map popped up on our phone screen and we could see where their vehicle was headed—streets, avenues, and all.

Over the next several days our coffee meetings took on a whole new level of excitement. We now had an app that would allow all 23 of us to know when one of us had a problem; and where they were. KC then took matters to a new level. He reminded us that his entire group of app developer friends across North America had been sharing the app with groups of people just like ours. KC explained that the Boomware app could be set to whatever distance we wanted to input: 1 mile, 100 miles, 1000 miles. He explained that if we traveled to another city in Canada or the USA, got into trouble, and hit the app, we would soon find that app users whom we did not even know would come to assist us. He said he and his developer friends had arranged for a cloud-computing company to record the data generated when we activated the app on our devices. We all agreed: Wow! We have something here. We can protect each other. We can look after one another.

A couple of weeks later, the app was put to the test. It was a Tuesday evening, 10:12 p.m. Suddenly our phones all flashed an alert.

What's Going On?

John, one of our group members, was a local retired businessman. Two individuals started breaking into his house through the back door. They used a wrecking bar to smash their way through the door. He heard the commotion, knew something was wrong, grabbed his smart phone and tapped the red button on the app. He next dialled 911 to report a house break-in that was happening right now.

Four of our group happened to be close to John's house; I was one of the four. Two of our group were in a vehicle; they were driving home after attending a charity group meeting. I was driving home from visiting a friend I had not seen in a while. The fourth lived less than two blocks away. He was watching television when his smart phone alerted him that John was in trouble.

No sooner had the intruders gained access to the house, than John surprised them as he came around the corner into the kitchen. John's wife, Heather, woke up, heard the commotion, and came out of the bedroom. One of the intruders punched her and sent her reeling. The other intruder was struggling with John.

Seconds later, the two guys travelling together in their car arrived at John's address. One went to the front door. Finding the door locked, he began frantically yelling and ringing the doorbell. The other ran to the back door just in time to see the two intruders come barging out. One of the intruders was flailing around with the wrecking bar. When he tried to tackle the intruder, the wrecking bar slammed into his arm as the intruder shoved him away. John's neighbour from a couple blocks away arrived on site and he too was also attacked with the bar; hit on the side of his ribs and pushed to the ground. Just as I arrived on scene in my car, I saw the intruders running down the alley. That is when things got really interesting.

The police arrived fourteen minutes after the 911 call. The officers brusquely explained they would have been there sooner, but were busy giving a ticket to a motorist who had made an illegal left turn. They said the motorist had stopped at a local drug store to get some cold and flu medication for his wife. He was in a hurry to get home, came to a red light, saw no other vehicles on the street and made a left turn on the red light. By the time the officers had written out the guy's ticket and made their way to John's 911 call, fourteen-minutes had elapsed.

When the police arrived, they were met with quite a scene. John had been punched a couple of times and was bleeding from his mouth. Heather had a bloody nose and lump on her head. One guy with a broken arm, another who had taken a blow to the ribs and could hardly breath. The police called an ambulance to take the four injured away. I and the gentleman who had initially been ringing the doorbell and yelling for John to open the door were ordered to make our way to the local police station to make a statement.

At the police station we were shown into an interview room. A burly Sergeant who had a neck the size of my waist and biceps like Burmese pythons started taking notes. He was very curious as to how four of us had all of a sudden known our friend was in trouble. We told the story of our coffee group, the app developer in our group, the Boomware app, and how it kept us entangled.

Then he dropped a bombshell on us. He told us in no uncertain terms that the app was illegal. We gave our heads a shake in utter disbelief. We explained that had we not gotten there as quickly as we did, John and Heather would certainly have had a much worse beating laid on them. We asked, "How in hell could this be illegal?" The Sergeant looked us up and down and coldly replied, "It is against the law to take the law into your own hands." I replied, "We were not taking the law into our own hands; we were merely helping someone who was in trouble!"

Nothing doing. The Sergeant was not going to be swayed. He reminded us that the intruders had a weapon and that we should not have interfered; we should have waited for the police! "But," I argued, "it took the police fourteen minutes to get there and by this time our friends could have been beaten worse and maybe even killed."

The Sergeant then eased into a long lecture. He mentioned this is Canada and that in Canada we should understand what the law is all about. He said that older people like us should be at home minding our own business! He excused himself from the table, saying he would be back in a minute. He walked out of the room, his frame nearly filling the doorway. He came back with a photocopied article in his grasp. He laid the article on the table and pointed out that this article described how Prime Minister Trudeau had recently said if you are on a farm or ranch, and someone is in your yard robbing you of your possessions, you should not take out a gun; you should lock yourself in your house and call the local RCMP or local police.

We reminded the good Sergeant that in rural Saskatchewan, farmers and ranchers are sometimes up to an hour away from the nearest police detachment. The rambling echo we got was "It's the law! You should not question the law. Prime Minister Trudeau has made it very clear that this approach is best for all Canadians!"

When we walked out of the police station around three o'clock in the morning, we had a renewed dedication to the Boomware app. As far as we were concerned, our age, our concerns, our desire to enjoy our so-called golden years meant nothing to the police. Sometimes when old people get upset, they will take action and do something about it.

CHAPTER 21

My dream then took on a bit of a political slant. I had images of Ottawa and the House of Commons. I had visions of Prime Minister Trudeau with a golden spoon in his mouth, blackface makeup neatly applied, standing in front of a classroom full of drama students. He was standing in front of a chalk board in the drama classroom. He scribbled some numbers on the board as he talked to the drama class. The numbers were startling: the federal debt was standing at just over $1.21 trillion as of March 2023. The numbers he was scribbling showed the government would have a balanced budget again by 2040. In 2040, the federal debt would be at $1.1 trillion because under Liberal leadership the economy would soar to new heights and the government would pay down some of the debt. He scribbled the word *inflation* on the chalkboard along with an arrow that pointed up. He scribbled the word *Boomer*, then proceeded to draw a diagonal line through the word. He scribbled the word *elderly* and then drew a line through it. He scribbled the words *social programs* and then an arrow pointing downwards.

What's Going On?

My dream drifted to farms and ranches in rural Saskatchewan. People on those farms and ranches not allowed to protect themselves, at least according to government. My dream then drifted to the coffee shop.

John showed up with his battered face. Our other two friends were there too; one with a broken arm, the other with broken ribs. The general tone of discussion around the table was that we certainly helped a friend, but a couple of us had really paid the price. In the end, who won? The two thieves; that's who. They got away unscathed and if they ever do get caught, will only get a slap on their hands.

Someone around the table asked if any of us would be afraid to do illegal things? My dream drifted to Manitoba, to Vince Li, to the 2008 beheading incident on a Greyhound bus. A guy on a bus stabs the passenger next to him, cuts the passenger's head off, and is seen cannibalizing it as police arrive. They escort him from the bus and take him into custody. After serving time in a mental institution, his record is cleared, he is freed, given medication, and even allowed to change his name.

No one on that bus had a pistol. And now, thanks to Mr. Trudeau, as of 2022, we cannot have one. Violate that law and you will be in deep shit!

One of our group, a guy we call "Uncle Ed," suddenly stood up and said, "I am 78 years old and have cancer that is internal and cannot be operated on. I still get around pretty good and have been robbed and beaten up over the years and have had police give me bullshit tickets. Instead of trying to help me, I get ignored, and I am tired of this. My doctor said in my condition—and he has diagnosed people in my state many times—I have maximum of three years to live. I will never be abused again. I am going home; I have a few guns and I have registered none of them over the years. I have not gone into all the government bullshit to get all the forms needed to even buy shells. I am going to take my Remington semi-automatic shotgun out to my garage and cut the barrel off as short as I can. I will carry it wherever I go—and I will never be beat up, robbed or abused again. For the assholes and criminals who want to take advantage of us older people, you come to my home and try it. I have something waiting for you. The party is over."

Maybe Uncle Ed had a point. We all had grown up in the late '40s and parts of the '50s. Times were different back then. One way or another, we looked after ourselves and our families. We looked after one another. People helping people. Neighbours helping neighbours. Common sense was the order of the day.

How about our grandfathers and other homesteaders and what they had to endure? My dream drifted to a story I had heard when growing up. A couple and their three young boys, left Ukraine in 1903 and boarded a ship to head to Canada. They came to Saskatchewan by train, purchased a horse and wagon and paid the required $10 fee to stake one quarter of land (160 acres). When they arrived at the location of their quarter section of land, they dug a hole, turned the wagon over, and slept in the hole until such time as a mud hut (a soddie) could be constructed. Imagine using the horse and a plough to break the sod, to grow a crop to feed a wife and three children. Can you imagine assholes, intruders, and thieves fooling around with this family? Over time, more homesteading families arrived in the area. Schools were eventually built; so were churches. These hard-working, God-fearing people all became a part of a community. Work was the key to it all; hard work. People worked, they toiled. People looked after one another; because they could. This is what made a community. People looking after people. People caring about one another.

CHAPTER 22

Uncle Ed was bound and determined to follow through with carrying a gun. In the following days, a few more of our group decided to do so as well. A few more people came out to our coffee meetings. KC loaded the app onto their smart phones.

Another test of the app would soon occur.

It was a Saturday night, about 11:00 p.m. Our phones all flashed an alert that Joseph had a problem at 1332 - 3rd Ave N.W. Four of us were in the area, all less than a minute away. Two men were in his garage attempting to start his vehicle. Paul and Fred were first on scene; within seconds of one another. They wheeled their vehicles into Joseph's driveway. Whoever was attempting to start his vehicle would now not be able to get the car out of the garage. The two men were trapped. When Joseph saw the two vehicles in his driveway, he came out of his house; loaded shotgun in hand. Seconds later another of our group, Arthur arrived on scene. They jumped out of their cars, guns held high. They hollered at the two men in the garage, "Hands up or we will shoot you." I arrived just after Arthur. I too had a gun with me, my trusted .40 calibre Glock.

Joseph had already called the police and approximately twelve minutes later a police car arrived with two officers. The officers looked a little shocked, not to mention upset; five old guys, all armed, holding two hostages at gunpoint in a car in a dimly lit garage late at night.

The police asked the two criminals what their side of the story was; where they had come from. They told the cops that they had been approached by someone who wanted to play a prank on a friend. This person explained to them that he would drop them off at his friend's house. He gave them a black-market device that would open the garage door. He gave them another black-market fob-looking device that would start the car. All they had to do was would go into the garage, start the friend's car, back it out and then park it a couple blocks away. The next morning, his friend would have a panic attack when he found his car missing.

The police did not believe this bullshit story. The would-be thieves then started to back-peddle their story. They said that the gentleman who had engaged their assistance had dropped them at the wrong address. They said the garage door had been open when they were dropped off. The cops examined the garage door and found no damage. Joseph argued that the car had been locked. So, how did the two would-be-thieves get into the car? They told the cops that the car had been unlocked. The cops than asked the two where the gentleman was who had dropped them off. They said he drove away when he saw a group of old lunatics show up waving guns. The two would-be-thieves shamelessly then reminded the police that there was no sign of forced entry, no actual theft, and a group of old guys had arrived on scene waving guns. They said this was a case of mistaken address identity, they had done nothing illegal and should not be charged.

The police took their names, let them go and advised the group of us to hand over our weapons. We were instructed to come to the police station to file a report. Just before 1:30 a.m. the group of us shuffled into the local station. Waiting for us were the two police officers and their Sergeant. He asked us to give our side of the story. He then asked the two police officers their side of the story and the story of the two guys who were in the garage.

The Sergeant made it very clear to us that there was no clear evidence that the two gentlemen who were in the garage were involved in criminal behaviour. Their story was that the garage door had been open. Joseph told the Sergeant it had not been open. He knew there was a problem when he heard the door opening. Joseph then explained to the Sergeant that on the floor of his car he had found a black-market device designed to help thieves start the ignition on a Mercedes car. He had also found a device to help open a garage door. The Sergeant seemed less interested in what Joseph had to say, focusing not on the two criminals but us five and our actions.

The Sergeant said the main problem in all of the night's events was five guys all being armed with guns. He reminded us that it was criminal to be wandering around with guns. He then asked the question, "Were your guns loaded?" He was very stern. He was not smiling. It was getting late, we were tired, we were stressed out. Paul was at the end of his rope. In answer to the Sergeant's question about guns being loaded, Paul sneered at the Sergeant and said, "It wouldn't have done us much good if they weren't!" We all kind of chuckled. Not the Sergeant though. He was getting pissed at us.

It was after 3:00 a.m., but he was not done with us yet. He asked us how it was that we had managed to all get to Joseph's house all within minutes of one another. We told him the story of our coffee group, of KC the computer guy, and the app he had created for our smart phones. We explained to him our concerns about being seniors in a society with rising crime levels. He appeared to understand, but his facial expressions still said he was not happy with us.

We told him that we were prepared to continue protecting ourselves and our group using the app and using our guns if need be. He scowled and shook his head disapprovingly. He leveled his gaze across the table at us and asked, "Did one of you say to these two men, if you try to run away, I will blow your head off?" Joseph immediately answered, "Yes, I said it to them. When they realized we were not fooling around, their tune changed."

Joseph continued, "There we were, five old guys, some of us with knee or hip replacements, arthritis and other problems. There they were, two men in their early 30s. They could have, and would have, beaten the shit out of us had we not had guns. Plus, the guy that dropped them off would have helped to beat the shit out of us." The scowl on the Sergeant's face look like it was a permanent feature. He was really not happy with us. He reminded us that the two police officers who had arrived on site were saying the two men did not seem to be aggressive. Joseph snorted, "Duh! Of course, they were nice. They were trying to convince the two officers that they were innocent."

Finally, the Sergeant indicated it was time to wrap this matter up. He made it clear that what we had done, showing up at a residence waving guns, was totally illegal. He said our guns would be confiscated and used as evidence and our written statements would be used as evidence.

The following charges were read out to us:

- Unlawful use of firearms, use of a cut-off shotgun
- Unlawful use of handguns, one of which was un-registered
- Transporting registered pistols outside the home to a location other than a practice gun facility
- Threatening the lives of the two individuals
- Developing an unlawful organization.

It was now near 4:00 a.m. The Sergeant told us we could go home, but in ten days time we were to appear in Provincial court to face the judge. We were told that court sits at 10:00 a.m. and that we better not be late. There we were, a bunch of old criminals, tired, stressed out, charged under the law, with a date to stand before a judge to face the music.

When we all met for coffee two days later, there were 30 of us all crowded into the coffee shop. Our story had made the local news. The local radio station was blathering about how five local seniors had been charged with several gun related charges. The angry vibe coming from our

What's Going On?

group was pulsing through the coffee shop. How dare the law enforcement system charge good citizens and let two would-be thieves walk free?

The sound of a chair shuffling caught people's attention. People craned their necks and directed their gaze to a corner table. A man rose to his feet indicating he wanted to speak. We immediately recognized him: Mr. Shumko, the well-known, feared, and revered lawyer. He had just turned eighty years of age and was walking with his cane, but was as sharp as a tack. We quickly told him the story of the app and how it tied us all together so we could look out for one another. He said there were two things he wanted: first, he wanted a copy of the app loaded onto his phone, and second, he wanted to defend us at our upcoming Court date. He need not have said more. This was a huge break for us. He had carved out his legal reputation by handling, and winning, cases where he felt an injustice had been done. One of our guys in our group whispered across the table that Shumko was like a bloodhound; once he got on to the scent of a legal case he would not let go. Mr. Shumko handed his phone to KC. With a few taps on the screen, KC announced that the app had now been loaded.

The next day, the five of us found our way to Shumko's office. We were shown into a conference room. Mr. Shumko soon arrived and we spent the next two hours going over the details of what all had transpired at Joseph's house. Shumko questioned us over and over again, looking for holes and inconsistencies in our story. He reached the point where he said he was satisfied. He told us that the next day we should be at the courthouse at 9:30 a.m. He would meet us there. Court would commence its session at 10:00 a.m. sharp. He said the members of our coffee group could be there, but they had to sit quietly at the back of the room.

On the day of court, we filed into the courtroom quietly and respectfully. The first few cases on the docket were impaired driving charges. Once the judge had dispensed with them, it was our turn. The judge called out the name of the police Sergeant. He stood stiffly at attention and remarked, "Present, your Honour." Although he was trying to conceal it, we all could not help but notice the Sergeant had a bit of a silly grin on his face. The judge next called out each of our names. As he did, we each stood and politely remarked "Present, your Honour." We glanced at the Sergeant. He looked pained as he tried to suppress his grin on his face.

The judge next asked who would be representing us in his Court. A loud squeak from the back of the room caused people to crane their necks to see what was going on. The judge looked up with a startled look on his face as Mr. Shumko walked into the court room, cane at his side. Mr. Shumko worked his way forward to where we were all standing. The judge immediately recognized Mr. Shumko. The expression on the judge's face turned serious, almost fearful. The silly grin on the Sergeant's face vanished. He was now stone-faced. The judge asked Mr. Shumko if he was representing us. The reply was, "Partly, your Honour." The judge now had a quizzical look on his face. A loud squeaking sound again arose from the back of the room as the large wooden door opened.

All I could think was *WOW*. In sauntered Al Milo and R.J.J. Smith; two of the best criminal lawyers in western Canada.

The judge shifted nervously in his chair and began clearing his throat like he had just eaten a hot chile pepper. He looked like he was about to go into shock. Mr. Shumko introduced the two lawyers to the judge. The judge nodded his head; he had never met these gentlemen, but there was no doubt he knew who they were and he knew the reputations they had. Mr. Shumko informed the judge that these two gentlemen would be helping him with the case. The visitor's gallery, including our coffee group was buzzing; the room sounded like a beehive. The judge pounded his gavel, a signal for the room to quiet down. The buzzing continued; he pounded the gavel again, this time more aggressively, yelling, "Order in the courtroom."

Mr. Shumko advised the judge that we would be pleased to enter our pleas to the Court. One by one, we looked politely at the judge and in a calm demeanor informed the judge we were "not guilty." The Sergeant, who was at least 120 pounds overweight, sat off to the side looking very unhappy. When we looked over at him, sweat was running down his face. The silly grin that had adorned his face was gone.

What's Going On?

Mr. Shumko addressed the judge, making it very clear he wanted this trial to be held as soon as possible. Mr. Shumko then further requested he wanted a trial by judge alone. The judge said the trial date would be three weeks hence, April 21. He agreed to Mr. Shumko's request for trial by judge alone. Mr. Shumko thanked the judge for his professionalism. Before turning to leave, Mr. Shumko pointed to the group of men sitting at the back of the room; our coffee group. He advised the judge that his five clients were part of this larger app-using group. He further advised that Mr. Milo and Mr. R.J.J. Smith had now joined the group. The judge's mouth dropped open. The Sergeant wiped his sweaty brow with the back of his hand. With that, we filed out of the courtroom followed by Mr. Shumko, Mr. Milo and Mr. R.J.J. Smith.

After we left the courtroom, the eight of us went for lunch and discussed the events that had just unfolded in the courtroom. Both Mr. Milo and Mr. Smith said they would do everything in their power to assist Mr. Shumko in his defence of us. They both indicated that this entire matter was a total injustice.

CHAPTER 23

The next morning at the coffee shop, we were pleased to see our group had grown to 41. KC was there. He had just added the app to the newcomers' phones. The air was charged with energy. We glanced at the big screen television on the wall to see the image of a reporter talking to Mr. R.J.J. Smith. He made it clear he had come to the courthouse to see justice done, that he was here to defend our constitutional rights. He explained he would be assisting Mr. Shumko as would another lawyer, Mr. Milo.

Someone in the group had brought a copy of the morning newspaper. The headline on the front page said it all: *Heavyweights Appear at Defence*. The journalist who had crafted this article had done his homework. He described the smart phone app in a unique way. His article used the example of a senior whose car had perhaps gotten stuck in a snowbank. The senior could use the app to let people know he was in trouble. The app could perhaps save his life. The article then went on to detail the charges we were facing and how the charges had come to be. The article said we would be defended by Shumko, Milo and R.J.J. Smith; all three who were semi-retired but still very well known, and respected as perhaps among the best legal defence minds in the country! The article concluded with the observation that the Sergeant and judge both had looked very uncomfortable as Mr. Shumko showed up in the courtroom. It wasn't just us who had noticed the discomfort of these two. The journalist sitting back in the visitor seats had picked up on it too. Now the media was reporting on it. We were ecstatic.

Discussion amongst our group turned to the topic of who would be allowed to get the app. With all the media attention, we were now getting calls from friends and even strangers who wanted to get the app and to become a part of our group. We discussed what the qualifications should be. We decided on the following:

- App users must be 65 years of age or older; there would be no ethnic, religious or gender bias.
- App users should use common sense. The app should only be used for serious situations that otherwise would demand calling 911.
- Responding to an app alert would be strictly voluntary; there was no obligation to go to the aid of a person.
- Responding to an app alert could place the responder's safety, and even life, in danger.
- App users responding to an alert must never use weapons in an aggressive fashion.
- Guns could be used only in situations where criminals were already displaying firearms.
- Criminals are defined as individuals doing something that at least 80% of the population would deem illegal.

Lastly, we decided that before getting the app, a person would have to provide personal information indicating occupation and reason for wanting the app. KC agreed he would build a simple website that laid out these parameters. People could read the parameters. If they still wanted the app, they could fill out an information form on the site detailing their personal information and reason for wanting the app.

No sooner did KC have the site up than applications began to flood in. A lot of people indicated they had some kind of disability and were not very mobile. Many were quite old, many were older women who just want to feel safe. Many typed into the reply form comments to the effect that they just wanted to be able to walk outside on a nice evening without worry.

This list of parameters, along with the fact that a website had now been created, was then forwarded to Mr. Shumko. He informed us that he would formalize these ideals and parameters on letterhead. He would submit the letter to the Justice Ministry, explaining what we were doing and the constitutional legality of it.

A few days later, Mr. Shumko contacted the five of us and summoned us to a meeting. When we arrived at his office, we were greeted by Mr. Milo and Mr. R.J.J. Smith. They had legal textbooks open on the table and had been locked in a deep conversation. In particular, they were focused on the old self-defence provisions in Canadian law.

They directed our attention to the 2003 version of the Criminal Code, Section 34(1) which says: *Every one who is unlawfully assaulted without having provoked the assault is justified in repelling force by force if the force they use is not intended to cause death or grievous bodily harm and is no more than is necessary to enable him to defend himself.*

They explained that subsequent revisions to the Criminal Code brought in the notion of belief. The revised and expanded 34(1) read: A person is not guilty of an offence if:

> (a) *they believe on reasonable grounds that force is being used against them or another person or that a threat of force is being made against them or another person;*
> (b) *the act that constitutes the offence is committed for the purpose of defending or protecting themselves or the other person from that use or threat of force; and*
> (c) *the act committed is reasonable in the circumstances.*

They further explained that in the older version of the Criminal Code, there was Section 37 which read: *Every one is justified in using force to defend himself or any one under his protection from assault, if he uses no more force than is necessary to prevent the assault or the repetition of it.*

They explained that the contentious point of this old clause was the expression "under his protection," which could be subject to varying interpretations.

They explained that sweeping changes contained in Bill C-26 (*Reforms to Self-Defence and Defence of Property*) which came into effect in 2012, were now what they had to focus on. The three points expressed in C-26 that they were concerned with were:

1) Was the force used (or implied to be used) reasonable?
2) Was there a defensive purpose associated with the force (or suggested force)?
3) Were the accused's actions reasonable in the circumstances?

They explained they were concerned that our smart phone app was outside the bounds of accepted practice and accepted reasonableness. They were worried the judge would perceive us as a vigilante group; a group of people who get together to suppress and punish crime. They were worried that our argument of being a group that sets out to help one another in times of distress would not resonate with the judge. However, they believed that we are the opposite of a vigilante group. We deem there is a threat against a person or persons and we defend—therefore our actions are reasonable in the circumstances, we are not aggressors.

The three lawyers decided they should seek an appearance before the Court so as to file an arraignment for everyone except Joseph. They wanted to first take Joseph into a trial by judge first as he was the home owner who had been broken into. They explained that on the charge of threatening the lives of the two men in his garage, he did not expressly make death threats. He said he would blow their heads off if he had to. On the charge of unlawful use of a firearm, he did not use the firearm as in the express meaning of the word "use." He did not discharge the weapon. His gun was a shotgun that did not have to be registered; he used it to suggest that he had the means to defend someone who was threatened. He was not the aggressor; his actions were reasonable. In fact, more than reasonable!

On the charge of belonging to an illegal organization, the Boomers are not an illegal organization. The Boomers are a small group of people, joined by a need to help one another in times of stressful situations. If a person suffers a fall in their home, they can use the app and fellow app users can be there very quickly to help. They can call an ambulance for you and do whatever it takes to help. Everyone has the right to protect themselves. If an app user is being threatened, and if the police can get there that is great. But what if the police are too busy? Why can a group of fellow app users not intervene to help?

Shumko, Milo and Smith then started discussing judges. They concurred there are some very good lawyers who become judges because they want justice done. But they intimated that in far too many cases, it is unsuccessful lawyers using their political connections who are appointed to the Bench. They became political hacks and render judgements that do not rock the political boat, so to speak. They hinted that the judge who would be hearing Joseph's case was just that kind of judge; a political hack. They had searched the legal databases and identified the various cases he had ruled on. They found out he was a member of the present political party in power in Saskatchewan. He had campaigned for the Party and was responsible for bringing in large donations. He had not been overly successful as a lawyer; yet here he was, sitting on the Bench.

CHAPTER 24

Finally, Joseph's court day arrived. The four of us and several of our coffee group were there, sitting in the visitor chairs in the courtroom. At the front of the room, we could see Joseph. He was flanked by Shumko, Milo and Smith.

The judge called for order and commenced the proceedings. The Crown Prosecutor questioned Joseph on the first charge. The exchange went like this:

Crown Prosecutor: "Did you threaten the two men?"

Joseph: "No"

Crown Prosecutor: "Did you tell one of the men you would blow his head off? Yes or No."

Joseph: "I did."

Crown Prosecutor: "Let the record show Joseph Barkely did indeed make death threats."

Crown Prosecutor: "Did you point your shotgun at the two men? Yes or no."

Joseph: "Yes, I did."

Crown Prosecutor: "You made a statement to the police which I have in front of me. When asked if the gun was loaded you said it would be no good to me if it wasn't loaded. Yes or no."

Joseph: "Yes."

At this point the gallery started to chuckle and the judge pounded his gavel and hollered "Order in the court."

Next, the Crown Prosecutor turned attention to possession of an illegal firearm; a sawed-off shotgun.

Prosecutor: "Are you guilty of this charge, yes or no"?

Joseph: "No, but you …."

The Prosecutor cut him off, indicating he was to answer yes or no to the question of whether he was the owner of a modified, cut-off shotgun.

Joseph hung his head and answered, "Yes."

The prosecutor then advised the judge he had no further questions.

Then it was Shumko, Milo and Smith's turn to question Joseph.

First up was Shumko: "Mr. Joseph Jones, did you make death threats"?

Joseph: "The two men were much bigger than us, stronger, meaner and we had no chance to overtake them. I am tired of abuse that we seniors must go through. I did not threaten them, I merely promised them that if they were going to harm us physically, I, uh, well, I uh told them I would blow their heads off. In reality, had one made a move at me, I would have probably pointed the gun at his leg and pulled the trigger and probably blown his leg off."

The courtroom cheered and again the judge hammered his gavel yelling for order.

The next issue was illegal use of a firearm.

Mr. Milo came forward and asked Joseph if he had an illegal firearm.

Joseph: "My shotgun did not have to be registered and under Bill C-26, a person can protect another person if a threat is perceived to that person. How else could I help a person in trouble? There is nothing saying I cannot use a gun. What would you suggest, a sling shot?"

The crowd cheered again. The judge pounded his gavel.

What's Going On?

Mr. Milo: "Let the record show that Mr. Jones was in his rights to have taken the steps he took."

Mr. Milo then excused himself and told the judge that Mr. Smith had a few questions. At this point, the judge's face took on a genuine look of concern.

Rising to his feet and stepping forward towards Joseph, Mr. Smith asked Joseph if he belonged to an illegal organization. Joseph explained he belonged to a group of seniors who call themselves the "Boomers" who help each other in times of great trouble.

Smith: "Are you overstepping anything the police could do?"

Joseph: "Absolutely not. When one of our group is being robbed, beaten, assaulted or anything of that nature, we hope and pray the police will be there first."

Smith then stared coldly at the judge and boldly made the statement that he had the Boomer app on his phone. He said, "Being a Boomer is in fact the opposite of something illegal. I am proud to be a member of the group." The judge , looking shaken, called a 60-minute recess break for lunch.

When the court resumed, Shumko tapped Mr. Milo on the shoulder and whispered that it was time to call to the stand the policeman who had arrived at Joseph's home. Once the officer had seated himself on the stand, Mr. Milo proceeded.

Milo: "Constable Brown, when you arrived at the home of Joseph Barkely, what did you see"?

Constable: "I saw five men with guns outside the garage, an open garage door, and two men in the garage."

Milo: "The two men that had broken into the garage, did you check if they were armed?" Constable: "No."

Milo: "Explain to the court why not"?

Constable: "The two men were not the ones with guns, the five men subsequently charged had the guns. Also, there was no evidence of a break in."

Milo: "Do you think the four seniors had come to the Barkely residence because they had nothing better to do? Yes or no."

Constable, nervously scratching his head: "I guess not."

Milo: "I asked you specifically, yes or no."

Constable: "No."

Milo: "Did you have to see physical damage to the garage door to determine whether or not there had been a break in"?

Constable: "Yes."

Milo: "What year did this take place"?

Constable: "2023."

There were some chuckles from the visitor's seating area.

Milo: "How are most garage doors opened today"?

Constable: "By remote control devices."

Milo: "Could these two men have used a remote to open the door, yes or no"?

Constable: "I guess."

Milo: "You are guessing. This, I remind you, is 2023. You are here trying to convict these men and all you can do is guess. Then I presume you do not know. You do not have to answer my question."

At this point, Milo excused himself and informed the judge that Mr. Shumko was going to continue the questioning. The Constable did not look happy at all and glanced over at his Sergeant. He too seemed a bit unhappy, beads of sweat pooling on his brow.

Shumko: "You were specifically asked a yes or no question. You were not asked to guess. I will repeat the question. Could these two men have used a remote to open the door? Yes or no."

Constable: "Yes."

Shumko: "To continue, earlier you said you had to have physical evidence of a break-in. Now, you are saying the door could have been opened by remote control device. Does this incident constitute a break in? Yes or no."

Constable: "Yes."

Shumko: "There seems to be some confusion here. On one hand, you said there has to be physical evidence of a break in and now you have implied there doesn't have to be. Am I correct in making this statement? Yes or no."

Constable: "Yes."

Shumko: "You found five senior citizens on site and two men in their early thirties. The five seniors were armed, and the two young, physically strong men had no weapons. Against whom was it easier to lay charges? The seniors with guns or the two unarmed men?"

Constable: "The men with guns was the only alternative."

Shumko: "The question was, which was easier? You must listen to my question. The seniors or the unarmed men"?

Constable: "I cannot answer that question. There was no proof that the two men were breaking the law."

Mr. Shumko then advised the judge that Mr. R.J.J. Smith would continue.

Smith: "Do we live in a democracy"?

Constable: "Yes."

Smith: "By arresting the five seniors, was this democratic? Yes or no."

Constable: "Yes."

Smith: "Thank you." Smith then advised the judge he had no further questions. The judge announced that the Court would be adjourned until the next morning at 9:00 a.m.

The next morning, when the Court resumed at 9:00 a.m., Mr. Smith informed the judge he wished to call the Sergeant to the stand. Once the Sergeant nervously took the stand and seated himself, the questions began.

Smith: "You issued four charges; we will discuss the first one—making death threats. Please explain."

Sergeant: "Yes, Mr. Joseph Barkely admitted to saying to one of the men in the car that he would blow his head off."

Smith: "Was this to an unarmed man?"

Sergeant: "Yes."

Smith: "Illegal use of a firearm was the second charge. On what grounds"?

Sergeant: "It is illegal to use a firearm, under any circumstance, to threaten someone or to point a loaded gun at someone. This could have resulted in a serious injury or even death."

Smith: "The third charge is possession of an illegal firearm."

Sergeant: "Yes, Mr. Joseph had a shotgun, and it was not registered."

Smith: "The fourth charge is belonging to an illegal organization. Would you explain please"?

Sergeant: "Yes, under questioning at the police station, we were apprised that a group of individuals, that we now understand is only men, have formed a group—they call themselves Boomers. We were led to believe they will arm themselves with guns. Our investigation had now revealed that not only do they have a website, but they have an app that can be loaded onto a smart phone. As far as we are concerned, these people are about to challenge the Constitution of Canada. For example, it is illegal in Canada to belong to ISIS. This group of Boomers, by taking the law into their own hands, are very dangerous. In addition, they all have firearms. I have been a police officer for many years and this kind of vigilante activity has to be stopped. It must not be allowed to gain traction."

Smith: "Thank you Sergeant, I have no more questions."

Mr. Smith indicated to the judge that Mr. Milo had some questions of the Sergeant.

Mr. Milo stood up and walked towards the Sergeant.

Milo: "Sergeant, please tell us your definition of democracy."

Sergeant, "Democracy is a system where people get to vote, set up rules, and follow the law."

Milo: "Do you agree that democracy is for the people, by the people, of the people?"

Sergeant: "I would agree to that."

Milo: "Regarding the charges you laid, would the 'people,' be in favour of this?"

Sergeant: "I followed the law."

Milo: "That is not what I asked. I asked if the 'people' would be in favour of the charges you laid?"

Sergeant: "I don't know."

Turning to the judge , Mr. Milo said that Mr. Shumko had some questions for the Sergeant.

Shumko: "We are very concerned about the way laws are written. Are you more concerned about writing tickets, or keeping the peace."

Sergeant: "Keeping the peace."

Shumko: "Two men broke into someone's garage. There was a black-market electronic device used to manipulate the garage door, which is illegal. There was another fob-type device to help start the car. You chose to ignore these illegal devices and you laid charges against the seniors with guns. Is this keeping the peace?"

Sergeant: "Yes, I followed the law."

Shumko: "Were your actions democratic?"

Sergeant: "I upheld our laws."

Shumko: "It is time we get to the crux of what this court is all about. We are going to further the whole challenge. In 2012, the Canadian government introduced new legislation called the *Citizens Arrest and Self-Defence Act.* Have you read the details of this act?"

Sergeant: "No I have not, as I have been too busy. I am following the law."

Shumko: "Let me enlighten you. Under this new legislation, which amends section 34 of the Criminal Code, if you are attacked in your home, you have the right to take action. Specifically, it is outlined that you can use force to protect your belongings and most importantly, yourself.

Sergeant: "But this does not apply to these five men coming along and being armed. That is why they are being charged."

Shumko: "Had you read and investigated this Act, you would have known it specifically lays out that Canadians can use reasonable force to protect their belongings and themselves."

Sergeant: "These five men showed up and were not protecting themselves. They were like a vigilante group."

At this point, Mr. Shumko scowled angrily and informed the Sergeant that several people in this court, including Mr. R.J.J. Smith, Mr. Milo and himself, were Boomers. Mr. Shumko raised his voice and tersely barked at the Sergeant, "Are, you are calling me a vigilante?"

The judge quickly intervened and advised the Sergeant he did not have to answer that question as it is was of order. Mr. Shumko, calmed himself and continued.

Shumko: "This is what the crux of their charges is about. You as a Canadian citizen have the right to defend yourself and take action. This I want to remind this court. You have that right, specifically if you are in danger. So, Mr. Joseph Barkely used his Boomer friends to help him defend himself. This, I remind this Court, is what this case is all about. Mr. Barkely heard a noise outside his house. When he stepped outside to investigate, he quickly realized the situation was not in his favour. There were two men in his car in his garage." There was a buzz in the courtroom.

Mr. Shumko continued: "So, under our constitutional rights, he is defending himself by being a member of the Boomers. Under his constitutional rights he did use force and the force he used was his Boomer friends. Under our constitution, citizens have the right to help and protect others. Are you denying Mr. Jones his rights? Yes or no."

Sergeant: "The law must be followed."

Shumko: "Is our constitution not the law?"

Sergeant: "It depends on how the constitution is interpreted."

Shumko: "Exactly, and we are going to prove in this court that we the Boomers are following the law, which is our constitution."

Mr. Shumko then returned to his chair and Mr. Smith rose to his feet. He took a step forward and launched into the Sergeant.

Smith: "The democratic principles set up by Mr. Milo and Mr. Shumko seem to collide with your views of constitutional law. The law you followed does not follow the principles of democracy. Is that correct?"

Sergeant: "I followed the law."

Smith: "Sergeant, do you believe our constitution has anything to do with our laws?"

Sergeant: "I guess so."

Smith: "These men are criminally charged, and you seem to already have doubts about our laws. You are now guessing. You are supposed to know what you are doing, to know the constitutional rights of Canadians, but you are guessing. You have criminally charged these men, and now in this Court, you are guessing."

Smith took a breath and continued: "I have a question for you. Have you thoroughly read the constitutional rights of Canadians, yes or no."

Sergeant: "No."

Smith: "Let the record show the Sergeant has not. I rest my case."

The judge pounded his gavel and told the court there would be a fifteen-minute break. With the break over, and the Sergeant back on the stand, Smith continued his grilling.

Smith: "I would like to begin by discussing the notion of democracy. Again, I will remind the court that we live in a democracy. Over the years our democracy has strayed, and we have to come back to reality. These charges relate to four people who found out that a friend was in trouble and went to help that person. True, the law says you cannot have a gun and threaten someone. Let's examine the word 'threaten.' If I walk up to someone and say, "I will rob you, shoot you, and kill you." That, is a threat. However, if someone goes to help a person or friend, who is in danger, and shows up with a gun and says, "I will blow your head off," that is not a threat. This is a statement of defence of others as well as a statement of self-defence. As we can see the definition of our democracy as laws have grown and can easily go in a direction in which opposes our definition of democracy and in this case the rule of democracy must rule. Suppose we took a poll of thousands of Canadians and asked whether this man be found guilty. Most level-headed people would say no! And that is what this law should be. Again, this is democracy, rule by the people."

Mr. Smith then advised the judge he would be discussing the *Citizens Arrest and Self-Defence Act*.

Smith: "Let's talk first about what is the law. Under the *Citizens Arrest and Self-Defence Act* one can act in defence of a third party. Even a person who is elderly has the right to defend a person who is in danger. But that elderly person needs some help in carrying out his defence. He needs an equalizer of sorts; he needs a weapon, a gun. There is no other way! Your Honour, I challenge this court to tell me there is another way. *Citizens Arrest and Self-Defence Act* also says that a person must believe that force is being used against the third party. When someone notifies you that they have a problem, they obviously perceive a threat. Our app allows the person perceiving a threat to notify others that there is a problem. I am urging you Your Honour to examine the *Citizens Arrest and Self-Defence Act* in this context.

"The *Citizens Arrest and Self-Defence Act* also says one must act with the purpose of defending and protecting. How could a person, in this case a Boomer, help a person in grave danger? There is, as you can see, only one way and that is to be in position to actually act defensively. Being armed is the only way for a Boomer to do so. The gun laws are inept, the criminals have guns. It seems the only people charged, are not the ones using guns for crime, but for defensive purposes. So, as this court can see, people have to be able to protect themselves. The gun laws contravene this constitution. This court must recognize that the constitution is the law and people can protect themselves.

"The *Citizens Arrest and Self-Defence Act* also says the actions taken must be reasonable. Well, your Honour, let's examine the term 'must be reasonable.' Mr. Barkely and his wife are seniors. They are not physically able to fight. Two young, aggressive, physically strong men invade their privacy and attempt to steal their vehicle. Mr. and Mrs. Barkely are, like most people, living in a democratic society. They worked, raised a family, and now in retirement, want to spend a few years enjoying the fruits of their efforts. Let's now say these four seniors had not shown up. Well, Mr. and Mrs. Joseph Barkely would have been in shock, their car would have been stolen and the chance of this car being found would have been slim. The police would have taken their statement and left it at that. Mr. Barkely would have gone through all the hassle of calling his insurance company, arguing with them as to the real value of his vehicle while the thieves get away. The thieves would have altered the VIN number on the vehicle, probably repainted it and shipped it to a waiting buyer overseas. In so doing, they would have made thousands of dollars. Sure, the insurance would have paid Mr. Jones a sum for his lost car. But at the end of the day, who pays for insurance? The citizens of this province pay for insurance. As insurance losses rise, insurance premiums rise. People who have worked all their lives and people who are now working are the ones who pay the rising premiums. What's worse, your Honour, is had the four seniors not shown up there was a good chance the Barkelys would have been beaten or worse. Is this democracy? Your Honour, it is time this game ends."

Smith paused and regained his composure.

He continued: "In our democratic society, I am more than sure that a good number of people would agree that these Boomers deserve a medal. Where would we be in society, in our free world, if we were subjected to people not helping people? This is what life in our free world should be about—people helping people. This is democracy."

Smith paused again, adjusted the lapels on his jacket, took a deep breath, and continued: "Next, we should ask ourselves the question—why do we have police? Some call police peace officers. Well then, what is it to keep the peace? Consider the following example: There is a loud party in your neighbourhood, people are drunk, and the noise level is extreme. What do you do? You call the police. Why—because they can use force, the carry guns, they can call for backup with more police and more guns. Let's take this one step further. Suppose the party spills into the street. A couple drunks decide they are going to kick in the door of your house. You are a senior, you are in no position to fight with them. If they beat you, your quality of life will suffer. You will be injured. The government of this country says we are not to arm ourselves. I respectfully submit to you, your Honour, we are not wrong in wanting to protect ourselves."

The courtroom erupted in cheers. The judge pounded his gavel so hard it looked like he would smash his wooden Bench. Mr. J.J. Smith turned to face the visitors seating area. He extended his palms and lowered his arms, a sign for the crowd to calm down. The crowd now realized J.J. Smith was in control of the proceedings, not the judge. Mr. Smith turned to look at Shumko and Milo. They had little smiles on their faces. J.J. Smith is on a roll. He was unstoppable!

As Mr. Smith was calming the crowd, the big wooden door at the back of the room swung open; two more lawyers quickly entered and took a seat among the visitors. The lawyers were Mr. Matthew Klino from Vancouver and from Mr. Belleneau from Quebec. Both had been retired for years and were not only friends, but also associates, of Milo, Shumko and J.J. Smith. They had heard about the case and had flown in to support their associates. The judge, spotting Klino and Belleneau turned pale, like he had seen a ghost. He looked like he was ready to puke. Beads of sweat started to trickle down his face. In his courtroom, there were now five of the sharpest legal minds in the criminal justice system in Canada. The beads of sweat were ready to drip off the tip of his nose. Smith and his two fellow lawyers could feel the momentum shifting.

In one final jab at the judge, Mr. Smith said: "We have a constitution. If we cannot follow the law in this courtroom then what do we follow? I am wondering if Canada is presenting itself to the world as a banana republic?"

The judge's face started to turn beet red. Before he could reach for his gavel, Mr. Smith boldly stated: "Your Honour, I request a 60-minute recess for lunch." The judge, struggling to maintain his composure, brought down his gavel down, breathing out a sign of relief at the same time. "We will adjourn until 1:00 pm."

CHAPTER 25

After the lunch recess, the judge resumed his seat and ordered the court back in session. J.J. Smith advised the judge he wished to call Mr. Maurice Belleneau to the stand. The judge reluctantly nodded in consent. The 76-year-old Belleneau is extremely aggressive. He is feared, known as a lawyer who will fight to the end when some perceived injustice has been done.

With some careful prompting by Smith, Mr. Belleveau began to talk. He eased into a story of what he deemed Canada to be about. He talked about how immigrants to Canada were brave enough to settle this country, fight for themselves, and help each other. In times of danger, they did what was right. If someone was threatening them, they did whatever they had to do to protect themselves. Government laws did not factor into their behavior. The courtroom was very quiet; the judge, police officers and Crown prosecution all looked horrified.

Belleneau kept speaking. He reminded the judge and courtroom that "during World War II ...."

Suddenly the Crown prosecutor found his "mo-jo" and sprang to his feet. "Objection, what does this court case of four men illegally using firearms have to do with the Second World War?"

Belleneau raised his voice and said, "Your Honour, it has everything to do with life. Are you going to deny me what life and democracy are about?"

The judge had a dishevelled, agonized look about him. He realized he was trapped. He pounded his gavel, looked at the Prosecutor and said, "Overruled."

Belleneau thanked the judge and continued, knowing he would not be interrupted again. He explained that in this day and age, 2023, in the eyes of the federal government, people cannot protect themselves. If criminals show up at your doorstep, you should lock your doors and phone 911. Criminals at your door can kick it in, in moments. The police will take many minutes to get to you. If you live on a farm, they could take over an hour. Yet, according to the law of the land if you have a gun, you cannot use it to protect yourself! He asked, "Is this Canada? Is this what most Canadians want"? His voice got louder. He then yelled out, "This is insanity! Is this what Canada being about? Is this really democracy? My cohorts have described to this court what the Charter says about our freedoms and protecting one another."

Belleneau took several deep breaths and regained his composure. His narrative turned to the war in Ukraine and the injustices being exacted by Putin. "The people of the Ukraine are peaceful people, like we are in Canada. Yet Putin is trying to conquer the country, killing innocent people, including children. The people of Ukraine are doing everything they can to get a weapon to arm themselves. Women are alone in their houses with their children, who are not in school because missiles have hit schools, hospitals, and orphanages. They want a weapon to protect what is left of their lives. If some Russian soldier comes to her door or her neighbour's door to try to rape her, she can put a bullet in his ugly head. Meanwhile, here in Canada the government wants people to de-arm themselves. This is sickness, this is a government disease. We need people to stand up and be heard. People in Canada should get out a map and look

What's Going On?

at our far Arctic north and see how close we are to Russia. Putin could be coming over our northern waters right now." The visitor's area started to cheer; Belleneau knows he has control. He continued. "We are trying to charge and give a criminal record to people who have armed themselves to protect their friends and neighbours." He was now yelling and pounding his fist on the witness stand. "These men should be getting medals for their concern and what they have done." The gallery was giving him a standing ovation and cheering. The judge was yelling for the courtroom to settle down, pounding his gavel to no avail.

Belleneau knew he had total control of this courtroom and continued yelling, "What the hell has this country come to? This court must respect our constitution even if our present government does not." The courtroom erupted again, this time into near hysteria. Belleneau glanced at the judge, the Sergeant and the Prosecutor; all were looking to be on the verge of passing out.

They had never seen anything like this before. These five men were legends of law. Their years of experience added up to over 200. They were dangerous! They had a history of taking on clients who were underdogs and felt they had been wrongfully charged.

The visitor's gallery suddenly erupted again. The judge started pounding his gavel, but it is no use. The chant coming from the gallery was "innocent, innocent, innocent ...."

Belleneau started to wave his hands in downward motion to settle the crowd down. After the crowd settled down, he very politely apologized to the court. Again, there was absolute quiet in the court. He continued in a very low, deliberate voice, "Innocent, hard-working people have been charged in Canada, now have criminal records, are actually afraid of helping one another in times of danger, but moreover are actually afraid to protect themselves." Suddenly in a dramatic flair, Belleveau then threw his arms up in the air. He screamed, "Is this what our constitution is about? Is this what innocent hard working people have to live with? Let's not lower ourselves to that of a banana republic. This is Canada and we have a constitution this country is supposed to allow us to be free. These men are innocent. This court has to follow what Canada is made of. Canada was made by people helping people. The verdict has to be NOT GUILTY."

The courtroom erupted again. The judge was pounding is gavel. It was useless. People were standing and shaking their fists in the air. Cameras were flashing and cell phones clicking pictures. People were frantically tapping their cell phones to upload images to Facebook and Instagram.

Belleneau signaled to Smith that he was done on the stand. After the courtroom had settled down, Smith took a step towards the judge and announced that the defence was resting their case. The judge, looking pale, and dishevelled announced that the court was adjourned for the day.

Two weeks later, it was time for the verdict. It was a Thursday morning, 10:00 a.m., and the courtroom was packed. Canadian news reporters were there as well as CNN and FOX news people from the USA. The judge called the courtroom to order and announced to the court that he had made his decision.

The judge explained that the charges that had been laid were laid against five men. The current case pertained to only Mr. Joseph Barkely, one of this group of five. The judge read his verdict, "In the matter of uttering death threats—not guilty." The crowd stirred. "In the matter of illegal possession of a firearm—not guilty." The energy level in the crowd started to heat up. "Possession of an illegal firearm—not guilty." The crowd was starting to talk now. "Belonging to an illegal organization—not guilty." Further more, the judge added, the court would be staying all charges against the remaining four men. "Court dismissed" he said, pounding his gavel twice.

The courtroom exploded. People were cheering, cameras were flashing. The five, old, legal minds all had moist tears in their eyes. The long-drawn-out process was over.

Outside the courtroom it was a feeding frenzy of reporters, all looking for a statement and a sound bite. The story would soon hit the major news networks, not only in Canada, but in the USA. Even the BBC in Britain would pick up the story.

The first man to answer the questions was Mr. Peter Shumko. He thanked the law-abiding Canadians who had gone public and online with messages of support in his efforts to protect innocent people. Mr. Shumko looked at the crowd of journalists. He said he wished to remind all younger Canadians to elect good people; people who will do good for this country. If you think their policies will be supported by at least 80% of our population, vote for them. He then thanked Mr. Milo, Mr. J.J. Smith, Mr. Klino and Mr. Belleneau, who had all come from across Canada to help settle this injustice. He said today's ruling sends a message to the people of Canada that they do not have to worry about protecting themselves. The days of worrying about being charged when you are being robbed, assaulted, beat up, living in fear, were over. It is time for criminals who want to inflict damage on ordinary citizens to be afraid! He went on to say that senior citizens in particular have been ignored and in many cases live in fear. He said this decision will bring seniors together. He mentioned that many people have been inquiring about the Boomers app and how seniors can be tied together. Someone in the crowd, who looked to be in their late '30s or early '40s, asked Mr. Shumko about women who live in fear. Shumko responded that the Boomers and the app developers would do whatever they could to help all people, all hard-working citizens, including women. He said that the Boomer group had been contacted by many people wanting to get the app. He said the Boomer group had also been contacted by retired lawyers and even some practising lawyers. He says that anyone the government wants to charge for protecting themselves or protecting another innocent person, will never be found guilty again.

As Shumko thanked the media, he began to step back from the throng. He made his way to where we were standing and said "People want to be free. People want to drop the word fear from their daily vocabulary. What you have done—you five people and others that helped you—you have made a huge statement to society, just watch it grow."

Suddenly, I stirred. My eyes opened. Wow! I thought to myself. That was one hell of a dream ....

CHAPTER 26

My chair was just too comfortable. The Sun was streaming in the window. I started to feel drowsy again. I drifted off to sleep and I began to dream again. Must have been that cannabis cookie. Damn, those are tasty.

One day Walter got a phone call from an old buddy in Saskatoon named Joe who asked him if he would like to drive a vehicle from Saskatoon back to Moose Jaw. He had just bought the car for his granddaughter, but needed to get it from one city to the other. He would happily pay Walter's bus fare from Moose Jaw to Saskatoon and had also asked a mutual friend, Fred, to join him on the adventure. Walter and Fred could spend the night at his house, reminiscing about old times, and the next day drive the car to Moose Jaw.

Walter and Fred, both in their early '80s, got on the bus. It was a nice sunny summer day. Birds were singing and both guys were looking forward to a little get-away. The bus had approximately thirty people on it. There was a mother with a couple of small kids, several middle-aged people, a man and woman with a teenaged boy, a few other kids and quite a few seniors.

What's Going On?

Fred owned a .38 pistol but had forgotten to bring it along. Walter on the other hand had a Rossi 12-gauge pistol shotgun with a six-inch barrel tucked away in his inside jacket pocket. If you put a slug in the Rossi, it would hit 1550 feet per second when discharged. Walter had had the gun for a while. When he first bought it, he took it out to a friend's farm, set up some old cans and plastic bottles, and fired it. It gave him a heck of a jolt. He then set up a piece of plywood and from about five feet away, fired a shotgun #2 shot at the plywood. The pellets from the gun scattered on the plywood pretty good. This particular gun was a single shot. Walter figured if he was in trouble, he would need only one shot, but he also had a #2 shot shell in his pocket, for an emergency.

The bus driver was a cool dude and after about an hour, Walter asked him if he could put on some good old fashioned Rolling Stones music. It was kind if ironic that one of the Stones songs being played was *Sympathy for the Devil*. Fred was on the inside seat by the window and Walter was on the outside aisle seat. Across the aisle and one row up from Nick and Walter were two men. One looked to be in his mid-to-late 20s and the man beside him looked to be in his mid-40s. All of a sudden, the younger man gave a very loud scream, "I've been stabbed." He had a short sleeve white t-shirt on and as he ran down the aisle toward the front of the bus, blood was running down his shirt and all over the floor of the bus. People started screaming.

Walter yelled out, "Everyone lay down." He stood up as the 40-something guy started waving a bloody knife. Walter reached inside his inner jacket pocket. As he did, he looked at the knife-wielding maniac. Walter tersely said, "Put the knife down." The man with the knife started to inch closer, getting to within about five feet of Walter. Walter quickly noted there was no one behind the man with the knife. All that was behind him was the bus window. He said to Walter, "I am going to stick this knife into your gut, you bastard. You are going to slowly bleed to death. What are you going to do about it?" He then slowly, menacingly inched his way towards Walter. In one swift move, Walter pulled the six-inch Rossi pistol shotgun out of his pocket, aimed, looked the maniac straight in the eye, said, "You will never remember," and pulled the trigger. The blast was the loudest noise anyone in the bus had ever heard. By this time, the bus driver had hit the brakes and the bus had screeched to a halt on the gravel shoulder beside the highway.

The sight was sickening. The 40-something crazy dude had most of his upper body chest area blown apart. There was blood and body tissue all over; the glass window that had been behind the guy was blown out. People towards the front of the bus were looking after the young man who was bleeding. Most of the other people had by this time ran out of the bus. Someone in the crowd yelled that they had just called 911.

Kathy, one of the younger women on the bus, had some nursing experience and was tending to James, the young man who had been stabbed. She seemed to be doing a good job with just the basic First Aid kit from behind the driver's seat. James looked up and said, "Whoever that old guy is with the gun, if I could stand up, I would like to hug him and shake his hand."

Walter Zurknowski was indeed an old guy. He was a Boomer. He immediately made a phone call to lawyer J.J. Smith. After listening to the details of what had just happened, Smith instructed Walter not to give his gun up. Smith suggested he tell the police exactly what happened, and that he was a Boomer. Smith told Walter that when the police arrive, they are going to want to know what happened. Tell the police you have your Boomer app on your phone.

The police arrived about fifteen minutes after the incident. People were almost in shock. A few had their hands over their faces to prevent from looking at the shattered glass, blood, and flesh on the blasted-out window. Fred was also outside the bus. Walter told him what Mr. Smith had just advised. Fred opened up the Boomer app on his phone. A man and woman officer approached the bus. When the male officer saw the busted-out window and blood and flesh on the highway, he said in a very loud voice, "What the hell is going on here?" A lady in the crowd said it was horrible what happened on the bus and she started weeping. The two policemen stepped up into the bus and saw the stabbed James, now partly bandaged up by Kathy. The male policeman looked down at James and in a rude tone of voice said, "Who is responsible for this?" James, kind

What's Going On?

of gasping, pointed to Walter and said to the policeman, "This man may have saved my life. If I make it or not, he is a hero."

From outside, a voice was heard, "The ambulance is here." Walter then grasped James by the hand and said, "You are a tough young man, you will be okay." The paramedics carefully checked James' stab wound, helped him from the bus and then put him on a stretcher. The ambulance then headed for the nearest hospital. As this was happening, the policeman went to look at the body. The police asked the question, "Who is responsible for this"? Walter told the policeman that he has his Boomer app on. The policeman said that was not the answer to the question he asked. Walter advised the officer that in fact that was the answer. On Walter's phone, the Boomer app had a split screen with the group of five lawyers visible on the screen.

The officer stared at the phone app and the image of the five people. Mr. Milo introduced himself and started speaking to the policeman. He informed the policeman as to who they were; that they were fellow Boomers who will handle any problems other app users have. Mr. Klino then weighed in, informing the policeman that Mr. Zuknowski was not responsible. The policeman said he wanted to know who did the shooting and where the gun was that was used. Walter said, "I did the shooting and I have the gun." The policeman then asked Walter to hand the gun over to him. At that point, Mr. Shumko told the officer that Mr. Zuknowski would show him the gun, but would not give him the gun.

Walter pulled the gun out of his pocket and showed it to the police officer. The officer dropped his jaw. "That thing looks dangerous. Is it loaded?"

Walter said, "Not much good if it isn't," and put it back in his pocket.

At that point the officer looked as though he was in shock. Mr. Belleneau next spoke up, giving Walter and the officer some instructions. "Mr. Zuknowski will give you his full statement as to what happened, we will be watching and recording his statement, uninterrupted by you or anyone else. When he completes the statement, he will not be answering any other questions. He has been under tremendous stress and the five of us will answer any further questions you may have."

Walter then went to the police car and gave the complete statement which was viewed by the group of five. At the conclusion, the police thanked Walter and asked him to wait outside the police car. The officer radioed for his Sergeant. He asked the Sergeant what he should do as this was a very unusual circumstance. "When I got here, people were outside the bus. The bus side window was blown to bits. When I entered the bus, there was a guy bleeding on the floor with what appeared to be a stab would. Shortly after, the ambulance came and took him to the hospital. Two old guys named Fred and Walter were standing there. I wanted to know what happened and this old guy named Walter showed me this Boomer app on his phone. Next thing, I was talking to five lawyers who seemed to know every word of the Canadian Constitution. I looked at the body; the upper part of the chest and head are blown apart. There is blood and parts of the head, neck and upper chest all over the seat and wall of the bus." He told the Sergeant that Walter and Fred said the dead guy was to blame for everything.

The Sergeant inquired if these lawyers on Walter's phone had names like Shumko, Smith and Milo.

The officer said "Yes, those were three of the five."

The Sergeant said, "These five men are dangerous, and we really have to be careful. They have everything on video."

The officer explained to the Sergeant that the lawyers had advised that a picture of the gun could be taken, but that Walter had to be left in possession of the gun. They said if I tried to take the gun, I would be charged. These five lawyers went on to say they would sue the police department if Walter or Fred had any problems."

He continued telling the Sergeant, "These old guys, seemed almost invigorated by the episode, almost as if they had a purpose."

The Sergeant told the officer to make sure everyone on the bus was looked after. Another bus had been called to come and pick them up. The Sergeant said he would go to the hospital to talk to the guy who had been stabbed and get to the bottom of what had occurred on in the bus.

The Sergeant then went to the hospital and asked if the young man who had been stabbed was in a condition to see someone. The nurse went

What's Going On?

to his room and told the Sergeant he could talk to the man; his name was James O'Leary. The Sergeant went to the room and introduced himself as Sergeant Vantoppe. He told James he would record the conversation on his phone. James reached for his own phone and advised the Sergeant that he too would be taping the conversation.

James began to tell his side of the story. He said "I was sitting by this stranger and was texting my wife. Not about anything specifically, just talking. I had been down by Estevan working on the oil rigs and I was really looking forward to seeing her and my three kids. They are nine, seven and five. After about an hour, this guy beside me gave him a poke and before he knew what was going on, I saw he had this long knife blade."

"Did he say anything?"

"Yes, he said, 'I am going to kill you and a few others.' Then he stuck the blade into my side; the pain was excruciating."

He continued with his story. He recalled yelling, "Help, I've been stabbed." He said he had on a white t-shirt, and he grabbed his side and his hand was full of blood. He stumbled getting out of his seat as he was on the aisle side, and the guy with the knife was on the inside. As he fell on the floor, he looked back. There was this older guy who was standing by the seat across from the guy with the knife. He could hear the guy with the knife yelling at the old guy and he could see the bloody knife. He was crawling towards the old guy. He could see the old guy pointing a gun at the man who stabbed him.

"My heart was pumping hard, hoping the guy with the gun could do something. He said something, but in all the noise and commotion I am not sure what he exactly said. I was pretty distracted with the pain. Then all of a sudden, bang! The gun went off and all I could see was a splash of blood and flesh spurting all over."

He knew by some sort of instinct that the guy with the knife was dead. He had never seen anyone shot before, but when the old guy's gun went off and he saw the knife-wielding sicko blown to bits, he was the happiest man in the world.

"How could you be happy when you just saw someone get shot?"

Too late, he realized he had said that last part aloud, but he was angry at the Sergeant's response. "How could I be happy? I will tell you how I could be happy. I have three kids and a wife. They will all be very happy I am alive and giving you this statement instead of being murdered. To be honest, I don't give a shit about this guy. Do you understand? He tried to kill me and if it wasn't for the fact that someone had the guts to stand up for me, I would be dead. In this country, no one is to be armed, no one is supposed to stand up to these criminals. Well, the law is 'phone the police.' Had he not been stopped so quickly, that fucking asshole would have had a heyday killing others. There were also kids on the bus. If it wasn't for the old guy ... Walter is his name, right? Well, if hadn't been for Walter, how many people would have died? I remember a story years ago where a guy on a bus killed someone, cut his head off and was eating it waiting for the police to come. A few years later, he was released and is a free man today. If the guy killed me and perhaps a few others on the bus, would he be free in a few years, perhaps to kill more people? I am in pain, I don't like your questioning, I want you to leave. But in my statement, I want to thank this old guy Walter. He is a hero, and we need more Walters, and I am going to share this experience with the rest of the world on all social media networks. Now get out of my room."

The next day, James' wife Angela and their three kids came to the hospital to pick him up. There were lots of hugs and James' three kids were all smiles. Angela said she would like to meet this Walter and give him a hug. James said he would try to get a hold of him and thank him for saving his life. He said Walter had a friend named Fred who was backing him all the way. He told Angela that Walter and Fred were part of the seniors' group called the Boomers. They had both heard of the group and decided to find out more about it. They thanked the doctor and hospital staff and left the hospital, hand in hand, and headed home.

My dream then deepened....

Gerard was 73-years-old and still in good shape. He had two grown kids, both who had completed their educated and were enjoying successful lives. His daughter Irene, now divorced, was a beautiful, highly successful woman. She called her dad a few weeks ago, saying a creep that she had met at a friend's social party a few months ago, kept calling her. On occasion, he had was waiting for her in the parking lot at her work when she would come out of the office. As she walked to her car, there he would be, asking her out on a date. She has politely told him that she is not interested.

Gerard told his daughter he would help her apply for a court order to keep this guy away. The court order did little to help.

One morning, at 2:00 a.m., Gerard's phone rang. It was his daughter. "Help, this creep Paul is going to kill me." He had gained access to her condo as one of the other residents was coming out. The door was slow to close and in a flash move, he had breezed through the closing door. He found his way to got to Irene's condo and kicked the door in. Irene was watching TV when she heard her door smash in. She grabbed her phone and activated the app. When Gerard saw the message on his app, he launched himself from bed, grabbed his semi-automatic shotgun and headed for his car. Irene's condo was a three-minute drive away. As he was driving, he managed to keep one hand on the steering wheel while using the other to call 911. As Gerard was speeding to Irene's, he could hear everything that was going on as Irene's phone was thrown to the floor but the app was still activated. He could hear the man's voice, "I am going to beat then rape you and with this knife, I will slit your throat; you fucking bitch, quit screaming!"

Gerald pulled up to the condo, ran to the front entrance door. It was locked, of course, but a blast with his shotgun and the door took on a very different appearance; door parts and glass shards were everywhere. Irene's door was the third one on the left down the hall. As Gerard ran through the doorway, he could hear Irene screaming and being hit. As he entered her condo, he yelled at the intruder, "Get the hell off of her. The intruder jumped off the bed and grabbed the lamp off the side table. He said he was going to kill Irene with it. He glared at Gerard, saying he didn't have the guts to pull the trigger.

Gerard yelled, "I don't have the guts—well I beg to differ." One well-aimed blast and Paul's right leg was blown off below the knee; just like I blew that signpost to bits when I was growing up on the farm. He was yelling and screaming and writhing around on the floor. Gerard aimed his cell phone at the writhing mess on the floor and started recording the sight.

The Boomer office now had this all on tape. Two other Boomers, Cal and Doug, who had been in the neighbourhood arrived at the condo. They saw this man screaming and hollering and trying to hold his hand over his damaged leg. Gerard removed the remaining shell from his shotgun. The temptation to place a more well-aimed shot was just too tempting. Two minutes later, two policemen entered the room, but Paul was making so much noise, Gerard didn't even hear the police officers arrive. Two ambulance attendants soon arrived and started tending to Paul, who was swearing and yelling about what a criminal Gerard was. Gerard looked down at Paul as the paramedics tended to his leg. "You, asshole, you wanted to rape and kill my daughter and you are yelling at me?" He took his shotgun, cocked the gun, pointed it at Paul's head and pulled the trigger. He knew there were no shells in the gun. The fire pin made an audible click as Gerard pulled the trigger. Gerard looked Paul in the face and said, "I could have blown your head off, but I only blew your leg off. I guess you aren't so tough anymore." The EMTs loaded Paul on a stretcher and left the scene.

The police aware of who the Boomers are, took a statement from Irene and Gerard as to what had happened. Gerard told the police they were going to go back to his place as Irene needed to be calmed down and the officers allowed them to leave.

The police officers got their Sergeant on the phone and explained that when they arrived on scene, a wounded man was yelling and screaming at this guy named Gerard. The guy yelling had apparently broken into the condo building in an effort to attack Irene. It was that Gerard had used his gun to badly wound Paul's leg. They watched as Gerard aimed his gun at Paul's head and pulled the trigger. Thankfully the gun was empty. They explained that Gerard had told them a short story. When he was a teenager, he had used a shotgun to tear a 4x4 road signpost to shreds. He told us that he promised his dad that if anyone was ever to hurt one of his family, he would shoot them. Well, some sixty some years later, he did exactly this while saving his daughter.

Back at the station, the officers met in person with the Sergeant. He explained that this Boomers group with their phone apps can legally protect one another as they have won a court case; they can even legally carry guns. The Sergeant advised the officers not to suggest anything negative to the media. The last thing he wanted was thousands of people protesting. The Sergeant reminded the officers that the assailant's criminal activity will be slowed down for many years, perhaps forever. He reminded the officers that had they shot the assailant, as Gerard had done, there would have been endless complaints of police brutality; the politicians would have buried the police service in hearings and investigations. He explained that as far as he was concerned, Gerard would come to regarded as a crusading hero, a saviour. These Boomer guys have public opinion on their side, and the very best legal minds on their side.

My dream went deeper.

Yes, guns—how else can we protect ourselves? There are other measures. Many seniors are buying bear spray, horns, baseball bats—and keeping these things in their vehicles or in their homes and even carrying them when they are going for an evening walk. A boomer named Pete made a device he calls a holding stick made from two used hockey sticks cut to four feet in length and joined at the ends with a segment of rope roughly twelve inches long. Pete had figured out from his farming days that this device worked great to hold a person; sling the rope around their neck and use the two stock segments to hold the person at bay. The sticks also worked well as a type of club. Bang a person in the knee area and he would go down in pain. When Pete showed people how to make one, some visited local hockey rinks in search of broken sticks. Others used old broom handles, some even used 2x2 lumber.

George made one of these devices out of two pieces of old broken hockey sticks. One night, George got up around 2:00 a.m. to go to the washroom. As he looked out his kitchen window, he saw a shadowy figure by his garage. The would-be intruder was standing on a pail and was about to break into the garage through the window. George grabbed his phone, activated the app, put on a pair of pants and quietly headed for his back door, calling 911 as he went. George was 71 and was in pretty good shape.

As he exited his house, he grabbed his holding stick. As he approached the side of the garage, he could see that the intruder had managed to enter the garage by the side window. He knew the thief would soon be coming out of the man door situated at the front of the garage and walking away with stolen goods. George stood silently by the overhead door, his heart beating, beads of sweat dripping off his brow. The holding stick was doubled up and he was going to use it as a club.. After about three minutes he heard the doorknob turn. The door opened and the thief walked out with a gym bag full of tools in his hand. The thief had no idea George was waiting in the shadows. George swung the stick as hard as he could right across the side of the thief's right knee. Whack! The thief fell, and as he did, he let loose with a torrent of screams and profanities. He screamed at George calling him a fucking asshole.

George gave him another clubbing on his leg and said, "You want to call me names?" The thief then raised a hand as if to give George the finger. George took aim at the raised hand. Whack! The thief rolled around on the ground, holding his hand in pain. Then George separated the two sticks and deftly wrapped the section of rope around the thief's neck. George held tight as the thief started screaming and trying to get free. George kept a real tight grip on the thief's neck. If the thief raised his voice, George would tighten his grip. He kept the thief pinned like this until the police arrived.

The Boomer app notified other Boomers and just before the police got there, Ted showed up with his .44-magnum pistol in hand; Ronald showed up with a baseball bat. If the thief yelled, George just squeezed the sticks a little harder from time to time. Ted pointed his pistol at the thief in a menacing fashion. Ted carefully positioned one of his feet on the thief's knee. Ted then placed his weight on the foot. Oops! That was the knee that George had whacked with the sticks. The thief screamed in agony. As Ted released the pressure on the knee, the thief was panting, trying to catch his breath. In between broken breaths, the thief said he was going to kill Ted.

What's Going On?

The police arrived in about seven minutes later. What a sight. Here was George with some kind of a device fashioned from hockey sticks, a thief laying on the ground; George applying pressure to the thief's neck, the thief yelling at the police to arrest these old fuckers who were abusing him. Another guy with a .44-magnum, another with a baseball bat. The police had never seen anything like this before.

The police asked George to let go of the sticks he had around the thief's neck. They hoisted the injured thief to his feet and took him into custody. They called an ambulance, and it arrived in about ten minutes. Once the officers got a closer look at the thief, they recognized him. His nickname was "Muscle." Muscle yelled at the police, saying he had been abused by these guys, and he was going to get them. The police intervened and ordered Muscle to shut up. Ted walked up to him with his .44-magnum, pointed it at his head, and said, "I am almost eighty years old, you threatened to kill me, I'll be watching for you." The police said Muscle would be charged, and that they had the situation under control. The ambulance attendants laid Muscle on a stretcher and loaded him into the ambulance, strapped to the stretcher.

The police looked a bit dismayed when George told them that they had each used their smart phones to video record the entire event. But there was little the police could do. The Boomers had taken care of each other, all thanks to an app.

A few days later, I was contacted by our lawyer, Mr. Shumko. He read me a letter he had drafted to me over the phone. The letter read like this: A court decision allows citizens of this country to protect themselves and, in particular, if firearms are to be used in protecting oneself or protecting another person or persons, it is legal to do so. If you are a member of the association of the Boomers, it is legal. By this court decision, the Charter of Rights and Freedoms of 1982 is upheld. The association of boomers is a legal entity, with law abiding citizens. This letter signed by the undersigned is to inform any officer of the law that by attempting to remove an object of self-protection of a Boomer is illegal. If this does happen, the officer who engages in this will be charged and sued and so will the commanding officer, as well as the police department. It is illegal to infringe on people's rights and freedoms that has been established under the association of Boomers. Mr. Shumko explained that he had been working with KC and that this standard letter would now be sent to everyone using the app.

Sure enough, three days after Mr. Shumko crafted the letter, we had our next Boomer incident. Mr. Jack Obleman, aged 83 had a knock at his door; two men were standing there saying they wanted to read his water meter. He felt something was not right and asked them for some identification. They started pushing the door which was already about a foot open, and Jack knew he was going to be in trouble because they were forcing the door open. He quickly went back to his living room and pulled out his .22 rifle and pointed it at the two men. "One more step and I will unload this gun." The startled men asked him if he meant it. They told him he should not have a loaded gun in his house. He coldly replied, "You two bastards came here to do me harm and if you don't get out now, I will do you harm. If you think I am fooling, try me!" They turned around and went out the door. Jack had no time to hit his Boomer app, so he immediately called 911.

The police arrived about thirty minutes later and quizzed Jack as to what had happened. After he explained, they asked him why he would have a loaded gun in his house. It was supposed to be locked up and what he did was illegal. He told the police that perhaps they should check the court case regarding Joseph Berkely and the boomer app in regards to an individual protecting themselves. He informed them that this conversation was being recorded. He opened up a documents folder on his phone and proceeded to read the letter that Mr. Shumko had scripted. Jack then raised his hand and motioned behind him as he told the officers the .22 semi-automatic propped against the wall was loaded and no one was going to take it from him. The two policemen looked at one another, perplexed and not sure how to respond. Jack looked at the two policemen and in a loud voice said, "No one takes my gun! Is that clear!?" He then provided the officers with a verbal description of the two thieves and told the officers that they should make every effort to arrest them before they hurt someone else. The two policemen advised Jack they were heading

What's Going On?

back to the police station to review his statements and that they would be back for more questioning.

As Jack watched the police car drive away, heading towards the police station downtown, he opened a couple of the social media programs he sometimes posts on. He typed up a couple posts and hit the Send button. Jack did not have a huge following on social media. But within 10 minutes, the Likes started to come in. In fact, KC started to notice a spike in the number of people requesting to download the app.

Another incident happened days later when Vera Smithers awoke at 1:30 a.m. to the sound of someone breaking into her back door. She did not have a weapon but she hit the Boomer app on her phone; the entire network now knew that she was in trouble. She then called 911. As she slowly walked out of her bedroom, everything seemed to happen at once. Lester, pistol in hand, jumped out of his car and ran to Vera's front door. He banged on the front door, yelling for Vera to open it. Two other cars then came speeding up. Tim and George jumped from their cars and bolted towards Vera's front door. Vera opened the front door. Lester quickly entered the house, almost knocking Vera down. Two intruders had by this time forced their way in the back door. The sight of Lester with his pistol shocked them; in a flash they turned and bolted out the back door. The backyard had no fence, just a trimmed hedge. Tim and George ran out the back door and gave chase to the intruders. All they heard was the snapping of branches and cursing as the intruders plowed through the hedge, scratching and cutting themselves in the process. Vera was crying but kept saying to the three Boomers, "You saved my life."

The police arrived about six minutes later and asked as to what happened. Vera explained to the police what happened and told the police the three men had saved her life. Lester, George and Tim explained to the police they were happy to have used the Boomer app to help this lady. They offered to come to the police station tomorrow to give a full statement. The officers said that would not be necessary and started walking back to their patrol car.

John McDee was driving down the highway just outside of town. His night vision was not the greatest. At one point his car got a little too close to the dividing line just as another car met him, headed in the opposite direction. The car did an abrupt U-turn, and quickly caught up to John. The car driver started blowing his horn, yelling at John, calling him a stupid old shit and giving him the finger. This went on for about half-a-minute. Eventually John came to a set of traffic lights and stopped for the red. The driver of the car following stopped, got out of his vehicle, and approached John. The driver tapped on John's window, telling him to roll his window down. John said, "I am sorry if I came too close."

The guy said "I am going to kick your fucking ass." He then reached for the door handle and swing open the drivers side door. As he swung the door, John secured a grip on his pistol beside him.

As the door opened wide, John pointed the gun at him and said, "Take one more step and I will blow your bloody arm off, you asshole."

The guy's mouth opened and said, "You wouldn't do that."

John said, "You threatened me—try me." The guy gave him the finger, turned around, took a picture of his license plate and yelled that he was going to call the police. He told John that he had better hide that illegal pistol. John just said nothing and drove away. Little did the guy know, John had his Boomer app on all the time, and everything was recorded.

When John returned home, he poured himself a stiff drink of whisky. About an hour later, John's doorbell rang. It was the police. The officers said they had received a complaint about his driving and about his attitude. They said they had a complaint that he almost ran into another car. When the other driver tried to talk to John, he had pulled out an illegal gun and threatened the man with it. John opened the app on his phone and suddenly Mr. Milo's face was on the screen. John quickly relayed the series of events to Mr. Milo, who in turn introduced himself to the officers. Mr. Milo then bluntly asked the officers who was threatening who in this incident. Milo suggested the police should charge the individual for threatening John. Milo explained to the officers that the pistol was not illegal; John would not be surrendering it as he might need it in the future. Milo advised the officers to have their Sergeant review the outcome of the recent court case involving Joseph Berkely. The next

What's Going On?

day, the officers returned to John's house. They informed him that no charges will be laid, and that he should be more careful with his gun. John reminded the two that he has been careful with guns all his life.

The next day Emma Greeves was in the parking lot of her favourite grocery store, and she opened the back door of her car to put her groceries in. She saw a suspicious man aggressively walking toward her. She grabbed her phone and put her finger on the Boomer app. Sure enough he grabbed her purse strap, and as he did, she pressed the app button. Well, immediately her problem was seen by seven Boomers in the near area. Neal happened to be entering the parking lot of the grocery store. On his app, he could see exactly where the problem was. He jumped out of his vehicle and before the man knew what was happening, he was tackled by Neal, 71 years old, 6 ft 2 inches, and 220 pounds. Neal grabbed the thief—who was about 25 years old—only to be told, "Fuck off or I'll stab you."

Neal gave him a solid punch to the side of his head. As the thief went down, Neal dropped another blow to his nose; blood started leaking out. Neal could see the thief had a knife in a holder fastened to his belt. By this time, people began to see notice the commotion and a not so small crowd was gathering. In almost no time, six other Boomers pulled up, jumped out of the cars, guns drawn. In the meantime, Neal put his foot on the guy's stomach, opened his belt buckle, pulled off his belt off and took the knife. Someone in the crowd had called 911. The police arrived in about five minutes after the incident. When the police got there, they could see the crowd of people, six old guys, all with guns. The police demanded to know what had happened. Emma was still in a bit of shock and by now some of the Boomers were using the app on their phones, taping everything as it happened. The police were told everything would be on file with the Boomers office.

Emma said to the police, "These men are heroes. I may have been stabbed or killed and I would have been robbed for sure. He hit me twice as I was fighting for my purse." The police took the statement and as for the six Boomers with guns, there was no negativity by the cops and no attempt to charge the six. They were only told to be careful with loaded guns. The ambulance was called, and the man was charged with assault and attempted theft. A local news outlet appeared, and Emma made sure she was heard.

The story made all the major news outlets and millions of people across the country saw what had happened. Monetary GoFundMe donations started to flow in to the Boomer office.

Henry, aged 84, was in a Walmart parking lot loading a couple bags of groceries into his car when a hooligan in his late 20s came at him. As he rushed towards him, Henry already had his hand on his phone and touched the app button. The thief pushed Henry into the back seat of his car before anyone in the area could notice. He showed Henry a long-bladed knife and said, "Hand me your wallet and get out your debit and credit cards." Henry knew that help was on its way and tried to be as slow as he could be so that the Boomers coming to his aid could find him. When the alarm went off, many boomers heard the distress.

Each Boomer sets the distance they wish the app to respond to. Some had it set for 10 miles, some for other distances, but 61 people heard Henry's distress signal and knew where it was and where the vehicle was going. In the direct area within a quarter of a mile and less, there were eight Boomers and they started to follow their screen to the Walmart parking lot. Ron was first on site and could see someone in the back seat of a car. Ron walked over to the car and saw a hooligan pinning an old guy down in the back seat.

The hooligan heard a voice say, "Get your hands up or I will shoot you."

The thief glanced over his shoulder and yelled back, "You old bastard, it's illegal to have a loaded gun."

Ron calmly said, "Let my friend out of the car or I will show you what a loaded gun can do. Make one wrong move and I will blow your bloody knee off."

The thief froze, paralyzed in fear. He slowly withdrew from the car, his hands in the air, shaking like a leaf in a windstorm.

The Boomer office had called the police as soon as they knew that Henry was in trouble. The police arrived five minutes later and were

What's Going On?

greeted with an old guy waving a gun and a young dude scared shitless. People were now milling around, and many had their cell phones out taking videos of what happened. The police looked around at the crowd and people started yelling to the police, "This man is a hero; he should get a medal. Turning to face the small crowd, Henry in a loud voice said, "I am a Boomer, and I am proud of it and all seniors should be Boomers." The crowd gave a loud cheer and were clapping their hands. Then Henry told the police, as he pointed to the hooligan, "He said he was going to kill me if I did not give him my credit cards and pin numbers." The police did a body search of the thief who had threatened Henry. He had no knife on his person. Then they looked at the back seat area. Again, no knife. Then the officer reached under the back area of the seat, felt something, and pulled out a knife. The police handcuffed the hooligan and loaded him into the back seat of the cruiser.

Nelly, 75 years of age, a small lady, was working in her garden in the backyard. She looked up and through her back window saw an intruder in her house. She realized she had a problem. She had her handbag with her and in it she had a little semi automatic .22 pistol. She also had her phone. She hit her Boomer app. People in the area knew Nelly had a problem. She went to the backdoor of her house and the intruder, seeing this small lady come in, had no fear of her. He had her laptop in his hands. She said, "Put my laptop down you thief!" She pulled the .22-pistol out of her purse, pointed it at him and said, "The police have been called, don't move."

He said, "You don't have the guts to pull the trigger." He started advancing towards her. She yelled at him to stop. He kept coming. She yelled again, and then bang, bang—she fired two shots into his right leg. His leg started to bleed profusely, and he made a limped, crippled dash for the back door, blood squirting all over. He knocked Nelly down and her gun flew out of her hand. Two Boomers were in the immediate area. Tom (72 years old) and Myron (73 years old). Both were in good shape, and they came running to Nelly's front door. Nelly was screaming, the wounded thief was yelling and swearing, trying to crawl towards the gun which had bounced across the floor. Tom jumped on the man and forced him flat to the floor. Myron could see blood leaking on the floor. He yelled to Tom to drag the thief out the back door onto the back patio so his blood did not ruin the floor. As they dragged him outside, he growlsed at them and said "You assholes leave me alone. Can't you see this bitch shot me?" Myron pulled out his gun and said, "According to my trusty .38 calibre here, you are lucky I don't put some lead in your head."

Nelly, partly recovered from the initial shock of everything approached Tom and Myron. "You guys saved my life. I think this guy was crazy enough he would have killed me." The ambulance arrived moments later and the paramedics start working on the guy's leg. About a minute later, the police arrived and see the ambulance attending to the invader. The policeman said, "What is going on here?"

The man yelled out, "This asshole woman shot me. I made a mistake and thought it was a friend's house and she came in and shot me."

Nelly, who was small, but had some wicked fire in her said, "This bastard would have killed me."

The police start questioning Nelly and she gave the officer the entire story. The police told her that she had gone too far. All she had to do was call 911 and wait outside her house.

Nelly got upset and told the officer, "If I had just waited, he would have been in another person's house, and maybe another by the time you got here. You are too slow. That is the problem today—people can't wait for you; we have to look after ourselves."

The police then turn to Tom and Myron and say they had handled the thief too roughly, dragging him out of the house. Besides, the wounded man says he was at the wrong house. Tom then produced his phone to the officer. The officer looked at the screen and saw five lawyers looking back at him. J. J. Smith identified himself to the police officer and launched into a legal lecture, saying, "It seems to us that you took the word of this criminal that he had made a mistake and was in the wrong house. That is the problem with the law today, the government wants to run everything and have control of people and instead of believing people like Nelly, Tom and Myron. It seems that the criminals have the last say." Smith continued his blistering tirade, "We as Boomers are here to help not hinder the police work. Whenever we get a call at our offices of someone in trouble, the first thing we do as a group is call you guys. Yes, the police, and if you are there first, that is great. But in this case, Tom and Myron were here within a minute and you guys took about 15 minutes. Yes, they dragged him out of the house, let him bleed outside. Who is going to pay for the stress he caused; who is going to pay for the cleanup of Nelly's house? Not this useless bum, that's for sure. Her insurance might pay, if she has the proper coverage." He then concluded, "For the record, this is J.J. Smith and if there are any problems with Nelly, Tom or Myron, we will be fighting this to the end in the courts. This I will repeat, is all recorded and this is time to realize that people have the right to protect friends, neighbours and other lay abiding citizens and themselves."

Nelly's story soon hit the local television, internet sites, and major news outlets. The story headlines were loud and clear. Nelly had a gun; she knew how to use it. She protected herself, shot an intruder and was saved by two Boomers who were in the area.

Joan Hamker was 85 years old and lived by herself in a little home on the east side of Regina. On a late Wednesday afternoon Jason, her early 50's son, came over and demanded she give him some money. She could see he was strung out on something, and she was scared. This was not the first time her son had approached her like this. She picked up her phone and calmly hit the Boomer app. Help was now coming. Outdoors was her elderly neighbour, Wally. His phone app alerted him to an incident. He soon realized the incident was next door at Joan's place. As he came up the front steps, he could hear Joan screaming. As he came in the front door, he could see Joan crying, sitting on the floor, leaning against her sofa. She was bleeding from her mouth. Jason was kicking her as she was screaming and crying, yelling, "Stop hitting me."

Jason saw Wally approaching and said, "You old fool, you need a good beating as well." Wally was 81-years old, and he ducked as Jason threw a punch. Jason then got off a knee to Wally's face. As Wally fell to the floor, Jason started kicking him in his side.

Kerry, 78 years old, was walking his dog two blocks away. When he saw his phone beep, he noticed the address to be 3431 Brown Street.

He picked up his pace and headed for the address. He had his .38-caliber pistol in his pocket. As he got to the front step, he could see Wally laying on the floor through the open door. He entered and took Jason by surprise. "Stop!" he yelled.

Jason looked at him and said, "Shut up, it is your turn for a beating," and came running at Kerry. As Jason threw a punch, bang. It happened so fast he had no time to pull the .38 out of his pocket. With his hand on the trigger, he fired the gun. The shell went through his jacket pocket and hit Jason in his right hip. The younger man went down screaming, "You fucking asshole!" He was now lying on the floor, holding the blood coming out of the wound.

Other Boomers heard all of this over their apps and called the police and ambulance. Less than two minutes later, two other vehicles carrying Boomers pulled up to see what was happening. One started to help Joan and the other Boomer was calming Kerry as he was held his pistol down by his side. That is the scene that greeted the police saw as they walked in. "What the hell happened?" yelled one of the policemen.

Kerry said, "This creep decided to give his mother and neighbour a good beating or perhaps kill them. When he came at me, I shot the bastard." Kerry set the pistol down and pulled his phone out of his other pocket. He turned the screen towards the officer. Seeing the Boomer app, the officer just nodded and turned away.

A few days later, the CBC contacted Joan to do a story on what had happened to her. She explained to the journalist her interpretation of gun violence. We grew up with guns on the farm. It was just common sense. The reporter starts to probe into how the government wants to see fewer guns and no pistols. Joan explained that she was living scared. Her son had hit her before to get money from her. She explained that she and her late husband had tried to raise him like most kids, but he got into drugs. It was his choice. "I tried to talk to him about it, but it was his choice and there was nothing I could do. Because of guns and now an app that allows people to protect others, we old people have meaning. I hope you people have the decency to air this and let people know. Let's get more people included in the Boomers, they saved my life! Thank you."

What's Going On?

At a Vancouver elementary school, a grade five girl outside for morning recess, could see a man getting out of his car with a large gun. She called 911 and shouted to a nearby teacher that there was a man with a gun. The girl had just received her first cell phone for her ninth birthday and her Grandpa had loaded the Boomer app on her phone and showed her how to use it. She hit the app button on her phone. Grandpa Bruce was a boomer at 79 years of age, and when he realized the alert was from his granddaughter's school, he started running, heading for the schoolyard. As Bruce arrived at the school, panting and out of breath, another Boomer, Lionel, pulled up and jumped out of his car. Both Bruce and Lionel spotted the man with the gun headed for the nearest entrance. They both yelled at him. The gunman turned and let go a shot that zinged over Lionel's head. Not 30 seconds later, another Boomer, Mike, pulled up. Taking quick note of what was happening, Mike took aim with his .38-caliber pistol and hit the gunman square in the chest area. Another shot echoed from nearby as a different Boomer hit the gunman in the stomach area. The gunman lay on the school playground, 100 feet from the nearest entrance. Dead. Within minutes the police arrived, followed by a SWAT team with an armoured vehicle. The school of about five hundred students, was in a total panic.

The police started taking statements. It turns out there were five Boomers on site, all of whom had guns. Two of those guns had delivered the fatal blows to the gunman.

The Boomers organization is getting to be very popular. Over 5% of the Canadian population are now members. Not all are even seniors. A good number are younger and physically able to respond to situations quickly. People in government know this is going on. They are aware of Mr. Shumko and his associates. They don't like it. But the people have spoken.

We Boomers are merely helping one another. We support the everyday policeman on patrol. Perhaps the bureaucrats should focus on the real big problems, such as the guys who are killing kids with fentanyl. Instead of wasting police time and resources giving a ticket to someone who doesn't make the proper turn signal, maybe focus on the real issues plaguing society.

Our organization is growing quickly. The question we are now debating is whether to identify ourselves. Should our members put a sign up at their homes saying Beware of Boomer or something to that effect? The government controls the media, yet here we are gaining public support every day.

Mathew Klino decided to do something bold. He found a radio station that aired a coast-to-coast syndicated talk show and arranged to host a two-hour call-in session to promote the Boomer organization. Once on the air, he said the number of seniors becoming Boomers is amazing. We have seniors who are getting together to talk about their safety. We have groups across the country getting together in homes and we have small offices being set up in many cities. Donations are now in the order of millions of dollars. Young people are starting to take notice of us on Facebook, Twitter, and other platforms. Our laws have to change, and it is good to see so many seniors going online, going public, and telling the younger generation of young people that we have to protect our country. They are telling these younger folks that instead of voting for a populist figure with fancy hair and cute socks, it is time that Canadians voted for good people who can make a difference in the halls of politics. We have to find good leaders, people who see the big picture, and simply do what the majority of people want. There is more to politics than just getting re-elected. Klino went on to say that out of 38 million people in Canada, you would think we could find at least 170 who can lead this country. Seniors make up over 9 million people in Canada. We deserve better. We need better. We came along after the great depression and near the end of World War II. Our generation impacted Canada significantly as it helped the young country recover from a war and depression. The politicians of today forget that this group changed the face of Canada in the international stage, increased the Canadian living standard and the development of suburban areas. Sadly, the government looks at us as a problem as we need more retirement homes, more medical expenses, and are no longer part of the labour force.

What's Going On?

And with that introduction, the phone lines lit up.

- A lady identifying as Gloria called in. Her husband, Lionel, had been at the recent incident at the Vancouver elementary school. She wondered how bad things would have been without Lionel and other Boomers arriving on scene so quickly.
- The mother of one of the school students called in. She was grateful for the Boomers. She said she wanted to drive to Ottawa and stare down any politician who was opposed to citizens looking after themselves.
- A woman from Saskatchewan called in with a reminder that the country had been built on people having guns for survival, hunting, and protection. She argued that the citizens of Canada must be allowed to protect themselves.
- A man from Quebec called in and argued against defunding the police. He said we need the police but we also need people using the Boomer app too. He said if there is a person in need in his area, he will help out without hesitation.
- A lady from Winnipeg called in. She expressed gratitude for the Boomer app and said finally criminals are becoming afraid knowing that people have the app on their phones.
- A resident from Vancouver called in and pointed out that Boomers driving their personal, unmarked cars are more effective than police in marked cars.
- A woman from Saskatoon called in and reminded everyone that a vigilante is someone who is out looking for revenge. A Boomer with the app is a someone minding his own business, but willing to help someone in danger when called upon.
- A man from Swift Current called in to ask why would any government try to stop its citizens from helping one another.
- A man from Ontario called in and said he lives in a small town of 6500 people. He had recently been broken into in the middle of the night. His guns are locked securely in a cabinet. Before he could get the lock undone, the intruders were in his

house beating him and robbing him. He said the government needs to wake up.
- A caller from Calgary called in to remind listeners about the Ken Carter case. She noted that the legal system is slow, but it is working. Carter is a former Calgary police officer who went on to found Carter Industries which morphed into an $80 million success story. In 2013 he and his girlfriend Akele Taylor were on the outs. Carter hired a private investigation firm owned by retired Calgary police officer Steve Walton and his wife. Carter paid substantial sums of money (at least $1 million) to have Taylor harassed. Walton and his wife were charged with criminal harassment. Three Calgary police officers who worked for the Walton investigation firm were convicted of nine corruption-related offences. In 2020, Carter was sentenced to three years in a federal penitentiary. His legal team promptly appealed and he remained free on bail pending an appeal. In August 2022, the appeals court judge said there was no grounds for appeal and that Mr. Carter should turn himself in to start his 3-year sentence.
- A woman from New Brunswick called in to say that on the entire subject of guns and people protecting themselves, it is time the Ottawa crowd got its heads out of the sand.
- A rancher from southern Alberta called in to tell callers he lives 55 miles from the nearest RCMP detachment. If someone decides to rob him late at night at his ranch, the government is saying he cannot protect his family. Who do these idiots in Ottawa think they are?
- A financial planner from Edward Jones called in to remind people to read their recent report in retirement. Retirement is not about resting; it is about finding a new purpose. The Boomers now have a purpose and the government had better get out of the way.
- A caller from White Rock, BC called in to express sorrow over the Ryan Grantham case. True, the young man had mental

health problems, but he was fixated on Trudeau. How sad it is that someone takes such a disliking to a politician that they decide to head to Ottawa to do harm.

After two hours of calls like this, Mr. Klino announced that he was out of time. He thanked everyone who had called in and who had taken the time to listen in.

Suddenly, with a startle, I woke up. Holy crap! What a wild dream! How much cannabis was in that cookie? I went off to the kitchen to make myself a cup of tea. As I was waiting for the tea leaves to steep in the teapot, I looked at the cookie jar on my kitchen counter. No. No more cookies today. Wow! What a dream …

CHAPTER 27

The next morning, I made my way to the coffee shop. Joseph, John, and Uncle Ed were all there. So too was the retired computer programmer KC. As I sat down with my coffee, I said, "You would not believe the dream I had yesterday afternoon."

I dreamed that the days of seniors having to worry about their safety are over. I dreamed we had reached the time when government was forced to allow citizens to make criminals scared. I dreamed that KC had created an app for people's smart phones. If a senior found himself in trouble from a home invader or any other criminal, all they had to do was activate the app and any senior from the area who was running the app would get an alert. Before long, a group of seniors would come to the aid of the person in distress. I dreamed that we all had guns and even homemade weapons. We got ourselves into a pile of shit with the cops and we ended up having to go to court. Our situation created a media shitstorm and that famous Constitutional lawyer, Shumko, agreed to take out case. We went to court and he argued the judge into submission. Next thing you know, what we were doing with the app and with our weapons was deemed valid under the Constitution.

The others at the table now had their eyes wide open. "Holy crap," KC said. "I have often thought about designing apps for phones, but that dream is beyond anything I have ever thought about."

John, Joseph, and Uncle Ed were all shaking their heads in unison. All Ed could say was "Wow!"

John said, "Right on dude, it's about time this messed up world changed. Seniors have to be looked after."

Just then, Joseph said "Hey, hey, guys … look over there. I recognize that guy. Isn't he that Constitutional lawyer, what's his name, um, ah, Shumko? Wonder what he is doing here?

A NOTE OF LEVITY

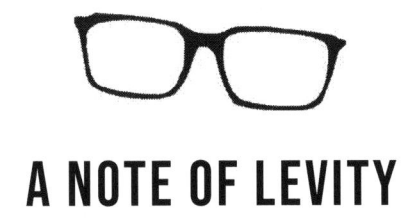

As I was writing this manuscript, I decided to take a bit of time off to regain my energy and focus. I got to thinking about how we have somehow lost our ability to laugh. This is a serious manuscript, but life doesn't have to be always serious. There is an old adage that says "laughter is the best medicine." Now that I think about it, maybe the medicine we all need is some good old fashioned laughter. We need to sit around with each other and tell stories. We need to tell jokes. We need to make each other laugh until tears roll down our cheeks.

All of this takes me to my good friend Nab, the practical joker. Nab was the best friend I ever had. Sadly, he passed away about 10 years ago. Nab was a gym teacher at a Catholic high school where I used to teach. His office area was small, with a desk and only a couple chairs. At the back of his office was a tiny, separate room with a toilet and a shower. If he wanted to have a laugh, he would ask one of the other teachers to come to his office at a specific time. The guest would no sooner arrive and get seated than Nab would excuse himself and tell the person he had to go to the bathroom. He would leave the bathroom door ajar about five to six inches. The teacher sitting in Nab's little office was practically right at the door to the toilet area. Soon enough the unmistakable sound of Nab starting to pee could be heard. What Nab had in the toilet area was a big, 2-gallon pitcher full of water. He would slowly start pouring a stream of water into the toilet to simulate the sound of him urinating. The sound of Nab peeing would go on and on and on. Nab would eventually come out of the bathroom with a sober straight face and tell the waiting teacher that he had not gone to the bathroom in days! It was hilarious.

Teachers began to use Nab's washroom. Often, they would not flush the toilet. The odor would make Nab angry. He knew this was all payback for his peeing gags and he did not like it. Once a month, the school would hold a Mass in the gymnasium. One day, just before the Mass wrapped up, one of the teachers made his way into Nab's bathroom. He left a horrible smell, and to make matters worse, he didn't flush. After Mass, the young priest who has never been to the school before disappeared. People thought he had left the building. Some of us went to Nab's office for a visit. The smell wafting from the bathroom was pungent. The bathroom door was locked. Nab started banging on the door, shouting "You stink, you stink ...." The door knob began to jiggle and the door opened. Out stepped the young priest. He looked at Nab, his face blushed, and was heard muttering, "I know, I know," as he hurried away. We laughed so hard we nearly fell over.

My favourite Nab story is the peanut butter dog shit story. A group of us would often get together at Nab's house to play card games. One time, Nab invited Sam, a teacher from school. Nab did not know Sam very well, but wanted to introduce him to our group. Nab decided to play a card game called Rummy. Just off Nab's dining room was a set of sliding doors leading to a deck. Nab's car was parked right under the deck. We got busy playing Rummy and had a few drinks in us. Nab decided it was time for a short break. Nab quietly disappeared into the kitchen and then went outside into the driveway. He put some peanut butter on his shoe sole and then walked around a bit so that gravel and bits of grass would stick to the sole. In reality, it looked like he had stepped in some dog shit. Nab was careful to take a chair next to Sam when we all reconvened around the table. Nab crossed his leg so the shoe with the peanut butter would face Sam. Linda, Nab's wife, knew what Nab was up to and said to the group, "Something stinks in here." Everyone looks around and Sam spots the bottom of Nab's shoe. He says to Nab, "There is something on the bottom of your shoe." Nab, calmly remarked, "I wonder if this could be what is smelling." We all knew what was going to happen next, except for Sam. Nab put his index finger right in the middle of the peanut butter, which had a bit of grass and gravel stuck to it. Nab brought his finger towards his nose. As it turned out, Sam had a very weak stomach, and you could see his mouth kind of open and he had this very funny look on his face. Nab then kept moving his finger towards his nose and he had this horrid expression on his face as it got closer and closer to his nose. He had it touch his nose and you could see Sam's mouth opening as Nab was really close to him. Nab then stuck this big gob up in the air towards Sam and in one motion, put it in his mouth. All of a sudden, Sam starts gagging and quickly gets up from the table and looks as if he is going to the bathroom. He makes an abrupt turn to the open door onto the deck, and we can hear him throwing up. After a few minutes, he comes in and starts apologizing as he tells Nab and Linda he threw up over the deck and onto their vehicle. Nab says to him, "Don't worry about a thing, let's play cards." Sam sits down and as he gets comfortable, Nab crosses his foot, points it towards Sam and if you can believe it, does the same thing. Sam jumps up, out the door, he goes and for a second time, throws up. We laughed until we had tears in our eyes!

We just don't take enough time to laugh anymore. We are all in a hurry to watch the game on our big-ass televisions. We are all glued to Facebook and Instagram.

We are hard-wired to laugh. We are hard-wired to have some fun. Let's get back on track before we damage ourselves further.

CONCLUSION

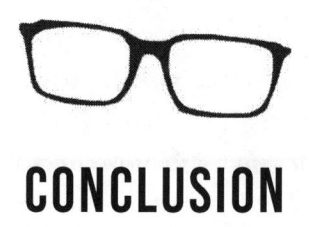

I have taken you on quite a rambling journey in this book. Actually, journey is too mild of a word. Let's be real. This book has been me screaming and ranting at how we are being governed. This book has been me lamenting at the present political situation in Ottawa. More importantly, this book has me asking the question over and over—what is going on? This book has been me urging people of all walks of life to wake up and smell the coffee! In my 74 years, the world has changed; Canada has changed. Canada continues to change, and not necessarily in a good way.

When I was growing up on the farm in rural Saskatchewan, we looked after each other; we looked out for each other. People did what was right by civil society. Sure, we had guns, but we respected them, we knew how to use them, we did not abuse them. But little by little, technology entered the equation. The family farm model began to shrink. A mass migration began that saw the baby boomer generation gravitate to larger towns and cities. The goal in migrating was to get a j-o-b. The move to large population centers saw us find mates. Kids soon followed. The population of the world started to balloon.

My perspective is that the human species is not hard wired to be living in crowded towns and cities; neighbours on all sides, neighbours above us and below us. As people continued to migrate, technology continued to advance. Vinyl records gave way to tapes and then CDs. Black and white televisions gave way to coloured televisions. Media became a tool for us to cope with life, the job we hated, the boss we despised, the co-workers we thought were idiots. And then came the Internet. Websites, social media platforms. We no longer had to read, write, and think. We just had to tune in and watch like brain-dead zombies. We could even express ourselves in 140 characters.

As humanity proliferated, the resources of the Earth came under stress. Society turned into a race for corporate profit. The profiteers learned now to manipulate our political leaders.

Eating fresh, wholesome foods became a thing of the past. Fast foods, artificially flavored foods, chemically preserved foods became the fashion. We are not hard wired to subsist on junk. Our mental health began to deteriorate. The mental health of our kids began to backslide. Next thing you know, the cell phone was introduced. This quickly morphed into the smart phone as the internet and social media appeared on the horizon. Expressions of rage and violence began to appear; slowly at first. The model of people helping people, neighbours helping neighbours was soon all but gone. Common sense was gone. The little family farms? Farming evolved almost overnight into a model of go big or go home. Farming was now all about bushels per acre, massive lines of credit, leased equipment, pesticides and herbicides. Petroleum products came into fashion. We soon found ourselves in a plastic and Teflon world. Our brains came under attack from the poisons we were eating, drinking, and breathing.

The world turned into a stressful place. The human animal was not hard-wired to cope with such stress. People started to lose their shit. Today, beatings, robberies, subway stabbings, thefts, and the like are commonplace in our crowded cities. Our society has been torn, divided forever. Those of means versus those without. Governments soon figured out how to implement new laws to micromanage society, especially that part of society that lacked means and resources. Governments of all stripes started convincing the masses that they could not look after themselves; government was the answer. Thanks to our *Charter of Rights and Freedoms,* the legal system started to go soft on offenders. The government of Justin Trudeau has worked feverishly to roll back the tough-on-crime laws of the Stephen Harper era. Nowadays, if you need something, just steal it. Defending oneself? Kick the shit out of a would-be-criminal and suddenly you were the criminal for failing to exercise reasonable force.

Media soon became complicit in all that was going on. Radio talk shows focused on the "game"; what was happening in CFL football or NHL hockey. Real news, the actual events in Ottawa, the actual geopolitics of the world became the stuff of the privileged class. The rest of the people could just watch the big game or the latest YouTube video.

Meanwhile, there was something else that was slowly creeping its way around the globe. In the 1970s, an obscure Swiss engineer started a management club in Europe. He urged companies to join. Ideas would be discussed; the future of the world economy would be discussed. The engineer's name was Klaus Schwab. He knew the Rockefellers in New York. They had started a similar club; their club was the Trilateral Commission. The Rockefellers inserted themselves into the healthcare sphere. What emerged was the World Health Organization. The family tentacles soon extended into the United Nations. Their overarching goal was to have a club of corporations, bankers, and select government officials run the world. Free and fair elections? Sure, go ahead and have them. Go ahead and elect governments. But the Rockefellers and Klaus Schwab would be charting the course behind the scenes. Our elected leaders will dance to the puppet master. These shadowy clubs finally were awarded the opportunity they long awaiting: a global health pandemic. Who knows where COVID started? We may never know. But, COVID allowed these shadowy clubs to spring into action. If you take the time to read the material on their websites, their goals are on full display. Capitalism as we know it is changing before our eyes. Agriculture is changing. Manufacturing is changing. It is all changing. Call it a re-set, call it what you wish. These two clubs are now in charge. Prime Ministers and Presidents are just figureheads. I personally knew three politicians that did care about our country and its citizens: Jimmy Gardiner, Lorne Calvert, and Dave Batters. We need 170 plus of these type of people to lead this country.

The COVID pandemic was perhaps the most divisive event in the history of the world. And if you think this outcome has been accidental, think again. Famed Chinese war figure Lao Zhu is famous for his strategy of divide and conquer. That's right, thanks to the divisiveness of the COVID pandemic, society is being divided and conquered. Aided in no small measure by internet technology, the media, corporate greed, declining food quality, and the stress of living in crowded conditions for which we are not hard-wired.

This latter part of this book describes a dream I had. I dreamed that senior citizens could carry guns or weapons to defend themselves. I dreamed that a group of seniors had fought in the courts using Constitutional arguments to win the right to self defend. I dreamed that someone had designed an app for their smart phones; if they were in trouble, they just had to activate the app and other seniors would come to assist.

Who knows, maybe one day this dream will all come true. One thing for sure is that the government has forsaken the common man, the everyday person on the street. The government no longer gives a shit about the masses. This is apparently the NEW CANADA. I do hope the country finds it footing again. I do hope my grandsons can enjoy themselves as they grow up. But, if things continue to unravel as they have been, then at least I hope this book will educate my grandsons as to why and how things have gone all to shit.

Thanks for taking the time to read.

ACKNOWLEDGEMENTS

I am grateful to the following people who, without their help and encouragement early on, this book may not have become a reality: Terry Johnson, Lynn Skelly, Verna Taylor, Lyle Hartley, Jim and Roseline Kroshus.

I am grateful to my editor in Mossbank, Saskatchewan for helping me with all the background research for this book.

NOTES

Chapter 2

1) First Nations group calls for security guard to be fired following violent arrest at Saskatoon store. CBC News. Morgan Modjeski, April 15, 2021.
2) Walgreens fed my family: inside the San Francisco stores closing over 'retail theft.' Abené Claytoni, November 15, 2021.
3) 6 Things You Didn't Know About "Shoplifting" Charges. Diana Aizman Esq. May 23, 2022.
4) Can You Get a Criminal Record for Shoplifting in Canada? Brian McGlashan. June 17, 2022. https://mcglashanlaw.ca/category/shoplifting/
5) Why Shoplifting Is Now De Facto Legal In California. Lee Ohanian- Hoover Institute. August 3, 2021.
6) Review of PC 459.5 Shoplifting Laws and Defences. D. Gorin and A. Eisner. Gorin Eisner Law. http://egattorneys.com

Chapter 3

1) Mental Illness. National Institute of Mental Health website. https://www.nimh.nih.gov/health/statistics/mental-illness.
2) Nutritional psychiatry: Your brain on food. E. Selhub. Harvard Health Publishing. September 18, 2022.
3) Dopamine Nation. A. Lembke. 2020. https://www.annalembke.com.
4) B.C. actor handed 14 years parole ineligibility in life sentence for mother's murder. CBC News. K. Larsen. September 20, 2022.
5) The Foundations of Lifelong Health Are Built in Early Childhood. National Scientific Council on the Developing Child. July 2010.
6) Violent victimization of Canadians with mental health-related disabilities, 2014. M. Burczycka. October 18, 2018.
7) National post-traumatic stress disorder awareness day. Statistics

Canada. https://www.statcan.gc.ca/o1/en/plus/1272-national-post-traumatic-stress-disorder-awareness-day.

8) The Age of AI And Our Human Future. 2021. Kissinger, H., Schmidt, E., Huttenlocher, D.Little, Brown and Company, USA.

9) When Gut Bacteria Change Brain Function. D. Kohn. https://www.theatlantic.com/health/archive/2015/06/gut-bacteria-on-the-brain/395918/.

10) November Estimate of Production of Principal Field Crops, Canada. Dominion Bureau of Statistics, November 1955.

11) Air pollution. https://www.who.int/health-topics/air-pollution

12) Merkel defends 2008 decision to block Ukraine from NATO. https://www.france24.com/en/live-news/20220404-merkel-defends-2008-decision-to-block-ukraine-from-Nato.

13) Russia Natural Gas. http://worldometers.info/gas/russia-natural-gas. Updated December 2022.

14) Natural Gas Facts. https://www.cga.ca/natural-gas-statistics/natural-gas-facts.

15) How much natural gas does the United States have, and how long will it last? https://www.americangeosciences.org/critical-issues/faq/how-much-natural-gas-does-united-states-have-and-how-long-will-it-last.

16) What Is the Keystone XL Pipeline? April 7, 2017. M. Denchak, C. Lindwall. Natural Resources Defence Council. https://www.nrdc.org/stories/what-keystone-xl-pipeline

17) Engineering a Deception: What Led to Volkswagen's Diesel Scandal. J. Ewing, New York Times. M Zeihan on Geopolitics. P. Zeihan. https://zeihan.com.

18) US Security Cooperation with Ukraine. https://www.state.gov/u-s-security-cooperation-with-ukraine.

19) Why Ukrainian forces gave up Crimea without a fight – and NATO is alert. P. Polityuk, A. Zverev. July 24, 2017. Reuters. https://www.reuters.com/article/us-ukraine-crisis-crimea-annexation-idUSKBN1A90G0

20) Oil and petroleum products explained. https://www.eia.gov/energyexplained/oil-and-petroleum-products. July 1, 2022.

21) 10 years after Greyhound beheading, family of victim and bystanders still suffering. CBC News. K. Pauls. July 30, 2018.
22) 11 Facts About The Horrific Murder Of Tim McLean Aboard A Greyhound Bus. J. Jeffers. September 7, 2022. https://www.ranker.com/list/facts-about-tim-mclean-greyhound/jen-jeffers.
23) Looking back at the Greyhound bus beheading a decade down the road. T. Bruch, A. McGuckin. July 30, 2018. https://globalnews.ca/news/4360713/lawsuit-over-greyhound-bus-beheading-in-limbo-10-years-later.
24) Vince Li, man who beheaded passenger on Greyhound bus, given absolute discharge. CBC News. February 10, 2017. https://www.cbc.ca/news/canada/manitoba/vince-li-discharge-1.3977278.
25) Please kill me, accused begs in court. Globe and Mail. J. Friesen. August 6, 2008. https://www.theglobeandmail.com/news/national/please-kill-me-accused-begs-in-court/article657590

Chapter 4

1) Hockey Canada dropped non-disclosure agreement with sexual assault complainant. CBC News. A. Burke, August 8, 2022. https://www.cbc.ca/news/politics/hockey-canada-sport-canada-complainant-2018-world-junior-team-1.6544919
2) Offshore Leaks Database. https://offshoreleaks.icij.org.
3) Hockey Canada facing backlash for survey on sexual assault allegations. CBC News. J. Tunney. https://www.cbc.ca/news/canada/ottawa/survey-hockey-canada-frustration-parents-minister-1.6589531.
4) Hockey Zone Plus: Tom Renney. https://www.hockeyzoneplus.com/salaries/31648-tom-renney.
5) Renney retires, Smith to become head of Hockey Canada. TSN Canada. S. Valji., April 20, 2022.
6) Standing Committee on Canadian Heritage. June 20, 2022. https://www.ourcommons.ca/DocumentViewer/en/44-1/CHPC/meeting-38/evidence
7) The Panama Papers Scandal: Who Was Exposed & Consequences. W.

Kenton. July 2022. https://www.investopedia.com/terms/p/panama-papers.asp

8) As Panama Papers dramatized for the big screen, issues they uncovered remain evergreen. M. Hays. April 4, 2017. https://www.globalwitness.org/en/blog/year-after-release-panama-papers-remain-evergreen

9) Paradise Papers – The Power Players. https://offshoreleaks.icij.org/stories/jean chretien. 2023

10) Paradise Papers – The Power Players. https://offshoreleaks.icij.org/stories/brian-mulroney. 2023

11) Revealed: Justin Trudeau's close adviser helped move huge sums offshore. Guardian newspaper. 2017. https://www.theguardian.com/news/2017/nov/05/justin-trudeau-adviser-stephen-bronfman-offshore-paradise-papers

12) Elvis Stojko took out $6.5M in life insurance on his parents and says he has no idea why it ended up offshore. CBC News. Z. Dubinsky. December 8, 2021. https://www.cbc.ca/news/canada/elvis-stojko-offshore-trust-belize-anthony-malcolm-1.6199821

13) Leaked files expose Jacques Villeneuve's multimillion-dollar tax dodges. CBC News. F. Zalac. October 27, 2021. https://www.cbc.ca/news/jacques-villeneuve-pandora-papers-offshore-accounts-1.6226467

14) The Canada Revenue Agency, Tax Avoidance and Tax Evasion: Recommended Actions. https://www.ourcommons.ca/Content/Committee/421/FINA/Reports/RP8533424/finarp06/finarp06-e.pdf

15) Snow Washing - Canada is the world's newest tax haven. Toronto Star. R. Crib, M. Oved. January 25, 2017. https://projects.thestar.com/panama-papers/canada-is-the-worlds-newest-tax-haven

16) CRA has identified more than $76 million in unpaid taxes from Panama, Paradise papers leaks. CBC News. E. Thompson. October 7, 2022. https://www.cbc.ca/news/politics/panama-paradise-pandora-papers-1.6609104

17) Trudeau, Pierre Elliot. Dictionary of Canadian Biography. J. English. 2007. http://www.biographi.ca/en/bio/trudeau_pierre_elliott_22E.html

18) The Aga Khan: 6 things to know about the wealthy spiritual leader. CBC News. N. Walji. September 12, 2014. https://www.cbc.ca/news/world/the-aga-khan-6-things-to-know-about-the-wealthy-spiritual-leader-1.2435214

19) What you need to know about the SNC-Lavalin affair. CBC News. M. Gollom. February 13, 2019. https://www.cbc.ca/news/politics/trudeau-wilson-raybould-attorney-general-snc-lavalin-1.5014271

20) The WE Charity controversy explained. CBC News. July 28, 2020. https://www.cbc.ca/news/canada/we-charity-student-grant-justin-trudeau-testimony-1.5666676

21) This is why Trudeau isn't being punished for his ethics violation. CTV News. Gilmore, R. August 15, 2019. https://www.ctvnews.ca/politics/this-is-why-trudeau-isn-t-being-punished-for-his-ethics-violation-1.4551354?

22) Conflict of Interest Act. Justice Laws website. https://laws-lois.justice.gc.ca/eng/acts/c-36.65

Chapter 5

1) Who was Jeffrey Epstein? The financier charged with sex trafficking. https://www.bbc.com/news/world-us-canada-48913377

2) The murky life and death of Robert Maxwell – and how it shaped his daughter Ghislaine. Guardian. https://www.theguardian.com/us-news/2019/aug/22/the-murky-life-and-death-of-robert-maxwell-and-how-it-shaped-his-daughter-ghislaine

3) What Did Prince Andrew Do? King Charles Just Evicted His Brother From Buckingham Palace After His Epstein Scandal. S. Hanson. January 26, 2023. https://stylecaster.com/what-prince-andrew-do/

4) Prince Andrew secretly visited Bahrain last week as personal guest of their royal family. Daily Mail. N. Anderson. November 20, 2022. https://www.dailymail.co.uk/home/search.html?s=&authornamef=Natasha+Anderson+For+Mailonline

Chapter 6

1) House of Windsor. Britannica. https://www.britannica.com/topic/house-of-Windsor
2) Ivan the Terrible. Britannica. https://www.britannica.com/biography/Ivan-the-Terrible
3) THE CONSTITUTION ACTS, 1867 to 1982. Justice Laws website. https://laws-lois.justice.gc.ca/eng/const/page-1.html
4) Governor General's Act (R.S.C., 1985, c. G-9). Justice Laws website. https://laws-lois.justice.gc.ca/eng/acts/g-9/FullText.html
5) Gov. Gen. Payette has created a toxic climate of harassment and verbal abuse at Rideau Hall, sources allege. CBC News. A. Burke. July 21, 2020. https://www.cbc.ca/news/politics/julie-payette-governor-general-harassment-allegations-1.5657397
6) Complaints against Payette include reports of physical contact. A. Burke. January 27, 2021. https://www.cbc.ca/news/politics/julie-payette-treatment-staff-rideau-hall-1.5887108
7) Nicholas II. https://www.biography.com/royalty/nicholas-ii MAY 26, 2021
8) The National Assembly of France: Creation, History & Impact. Study.com website. September 23, 2021. https://study.com/academy/lesson/the-national-assembly-of-france.html
9) Mary Simon. Canadian Encyclopdia. J. Boyko. September 10, 2021. https://www.thecanadianencyclopedia.ca/en/article/mary-simon.
10) Governor general salary increased by almost $40K during pandemic. R. Thorpe. February 7, 2023. Taxpayers Federation. https://www.taxpayer.com/newsroom/governor-general-salary-increased-by-almost-40k-during-pandemic.

Chapter 7

1) Bubonic Plague: The First Pandemic. Science Museum website. April 25, 2019. https://www.sciencemuseum.org.uk/objects-and-stories/medicine/bubonic-plague-first-pandemic

2) 1918 Pandemic (H1N1 virus). CDC website. https://www.cdc.gov/flu/pandemic-resources/1918-pandemic-h1n1.html
3) Plague. World Health Organization. July 7, 2022. https://www.who.int/news-room/fact-sheets/detail/plague
4) Don't Kill the Messenger RNA. Salk Institute website. February 14, 2017. https://www.salk.edu/news-release/dont-kill-messenger-rna
5) Convoy organizer Tamara Lich accused of having a 'selective' memory of whether she was told to leave protest. CBC News. C. Tunney. https://www.cbc.ca/news/politics/tamara-lich-mackenzie-bulford-1.6640630
6) COVID-19 vaccine mandate 'not an issue at all', trucking company TFI says. Global News. C. Reynolds. February 8, 2022. https://globalnews.ca/news/8604381/covid-vaccine-mandate-truckers-tfi/
7) Emergencies Act passes crucial House of Commons vote with NDP support. CBC News. D. Major. February 22, 2022. https://www.cbc.ca/news/politics/trudeau-emergencies-act-vote-1.6359243
8) Six Things You Need to Know About Bill C-69, Canada's Impact Assessment Act (IAA). A. Calder. Golder Associates., August 26, 2019. https://www.golder.com/insights/six-things-you-need-to-know-about-bill-c69-canadas-impact-assessment-act-iaa/
9) Tamara Lich's lawyer says pretrial detainment for minor breach is 'extremely disappointing'. Law Times. A. Oromoni. August 3, 2022. https://www.lawtimesnews.com/practice-areas/criminal/tamara-lichs-lawyer-says-pretrial-detainment-for-minor-breach-is-extremely-disappointing/368723
10) Federal government invokes Emergencies Act for first time ever in response to protests, blockades. CBC News. C. Tunney. February 14, 2022. https://www.cbc.ca/news/politics/trudeau-premiers-cabinet-1.6350734
11) Constitution Act, 1982. Canadian Encyclopedia. February 6, 2012. https://www.thecanadianencyclopedia.ca/en/article/constitution-act-1982
12) Ottawa needs support from majority of provinces to guarantee Quebec's share of Commons seats. CBC News. J. Bryden. November

5, 2021. https://www.cbc.ca/news/politics/parliament-quebec-seats-1.6238756
13) Jagmeet Singh. Canadian Encyclopedia. Tabitha Marshall, John Boyko, Andrew McIntosh. December 7, 2017. https://www.thecanadianencyclopedia.ca/en/article/jagmeet-singh

Chapter 8

1) From the archives: Meet Omar Khadr's two Edmonton lawyers. Edmonton Journal. May 2, 2010. https://edmontonjournal.com/news/local-news/from-the-archives-meet-omar-khadrs-two-edmonton-lawyers.
2) Key events in the OmarKhadr case. CBC News. September 30, 2012. https://www.cbc.ca/news/canada/key-events-in-the-omar-khadr-case-1.1153759
3) Omar Khadr. The continuing scandal of illegal detention and torture in Guantánamo Bay. Lawyers Rights Watch Canada. F. McLaren. June 2008. https://www.lrwc.org/ws/wp-content/uploads/2012/03/Omar.Ahmed_.Khadr_.Fact_.Summary.June_.1.08.pdf

Chapter 9

1) One suspect found dead, the other remains at large, following mass stabbing in Canada. E. Bowman. NPR. September 5, 2022. https://www.npr.org/2022/09/04/1121083048/stabbing-attack-canada-saskatchewan
2) Exclusive: Saskatchewan stabbing suspect's wife says she called RCMP 24 hours before murders. A. Stewart. Global News. September 24, 2022. https://globalnews.ca/news/9148025/saskatchewan-stabbings-skye-sanderson/
3) RCMP say Myles Sanderson,suspect in Saskatchewan stabbing rampage, died in custody after 'medical distress'. Toronto Star. September 7, 2022. A. Boyd, O. Mosleh. https://www.thestar.com/

news/canada/2022/09/07/it-still-feels-like-a-nightmare-family-members-of-stabbing-victims-on-james-smith-cree-nation-speak

Chapter 10

1) Crime and Abuse Against Seniors: A Review of the Research Literature With Special Reference to the Canadian Situation. Government of Canada. December 2018. https://www.justice.gc.ca/eng/rp-pr/cj-jp/fv-vf/crim/sum-som.html
2) Here is where Saskatchewan ranked among homicides in Canada in 2021. CTV News. L. Simard. November 24, 2022. https://regina.ctvnews.ca/here-is-where-saskatchewan-ranked-among-homicides-in-canada-in-2021-1.6167377
3) Moose Jaw's crime rate ranked 37th nationally in 2021, data shows. J. Antonio. Moose Jaw Today. https://www.moosejawtoday.com/local-news/moose-jaws-crime-rate-ranked-37th-nationally-in-2021-data-shows-5654825
4) Regina and Saskatoon fifth and sixth in Canada's Crime Severity Index. L. Schick. CKOM News. December 22, 2022. https://www.ckom.com/2022/08/02/regina-and-saskatoon-fifth-and-sixth-in-canadas-crime-severity-index/

Chapter 11

1) Criminal Code, Section 34. https://laws-lois.justice.gc.ca/eng/acts/c-46/section-34-20030101.html#:~:text=34%20(1)%20Every%20one%20who,enable%20him%20to%20defend%20himself.
2) Elie Wiesel, Nobel Prize acceptance speech 1986. https://www.nobelprize.org/prizes/peace/1986/wiesel/lecture/
3) Matt Gurney: Ian Thomson acquitted after shooting at his attackers. National Post. M. Gurney. January 4, 2013. https://nationalpost.com/opinion/matt-gurney-after-two-years-judge-acquits-man-who-defended-himself-with-a-gun

Chapter 12

1) Google CEO, US executives disregard summons to appear before House of Commons committee. National Post. Anja Karadeglija. March 3, 2023. https://nationalpost.com/news/politics/google-ceo-u-s-executives-disregard-canada-committee-summons.
2) CBC Paid Its Employees $16 million in bonuses in 2022. National Post. B. Passifume. https://nationalpost.com/news/canada/cbc-employees-paid-16-million-bonuses-2022
3) Canadian Taxpayers Federation. www.taxpapyer.com and www.debtclock.ca

Chapter 13

1) Nikita Khrushchev at the National Press Club, September 16, 1959 https://www.loc.gov/rr/record/pressclub/pdf/NikitaKhrushchev.pdf
2) Remember Khrushchev's Prediction in 1959? F. Updike. Culpepper Times. March 4, 2021. https://www.insidenova.com/culpeper/commentary-remember-khrushchev-s-prediction-in-1959/article_ec0cce4e-7d02-11eb-91ea-abdc2533a441.html
3) There are just nine steps from freedom to socialism to societal breakdown. FOX News. March 16, 2019. Tom Del Beccaro. https://www.foxnews.com/opinion/there-are-just-nine-steps-from-freedom-to-socialism-to-societal-breakdown
4) Payment Delinquencies Increase, Credit Card Demand and Balances are Rising. December 2022. https://assets.equifax.com/assets/canada/english/consumer-trends-q3-report-en.pdf.
5) Fed-up with crime, civilian group starts patrolling the streets in Dawson Creek, B.C. Global News. E. McSheffrey, E. Agahi. January 13, 2023. https://globalnews.ca/news/9409957/dawson-creek-bc-civilian-crime-response-group/

Chapter 14

1) McCaul's Final Report: The Origins of the Global Pandemic, Including the Roles of the CCP & WHO. Michael T. McCaul. https://foreignaffairs.house.gov/finalcovid-19pandemicoriginsreport/

Chapter 15

1) The Rockefeller Foundation. WHO website. https://www.who.int/about/funding/contributors/the-rockefeller-foundation
2) Rockefeller Foundation. Influence Watch website. https://www.influencewatch.org/non-profit/rockefeller-foundation/
3) World Economic Forum website. https://www.weforum.org/
4) Rothschild Family. Britannica.com. https://www.britannica.com/topic/Rothschild-family
5) WHO Constitution. https://www.who.int/about/governance/constitution
6) The First Ten Years of the World Health Organization. https://www.who.int/publications/i/item/9789241560146

Chapter 16

1) Trends in firearm-related violent crime in Canada, 2009 to 2020. M. Allen. Canadian Centre for Justice and Community Safety Statistics. https://www150.statcan.gc.ca/n1/pub/85-002-x/2022001/article/00009-eng.htm
2) Criminal Code section 84, Criminal Code (R.S.C., 1985, c. C-46), Justice Laws website. https://laws-lois.justice.gc.ca/eng/acts/C-46/section-84.html
3) Criminal Code section 95, Criminal Code (R.S.C., 1985, c. C-46), Justice Laws website. https://laws-lois.justice.gc.ca/eng/acts/c-46/section-95.html
4) Bill C-21. House of Commons. https://www.parl.ca/DocumentViewer/en/44-1/bill/C-21/first-reading.

5) No body, no parole: How the killing of an elderly couple led to the push for a new Canadian law. Toronto Star. R. Saba. January 26, 2020. https://www.thestar.com/news/canada/2020/01/26/no-body-no-parole-how-the-killing-of-an-elderly-couple-led-to-the-push-for-a-new-canadian-law.html.
6) The Three Legal Classes of Firearms in Canada. FirearmsTraining website. http://www.fircarmstraining.ca/classcs.htm

Chapter 17

1) Charter of Rights and Freedoms. https://www.cga.ct.gov/ S. Norman-Eady, January 1998.
2) Criminal Code section 33, Criminal Code (R.S.C., 1985, c. C-46), Justice Laws website. https://laws-lois.justice.gc.ca/eng/acts/C-46/section-33.1.html
3) Mental state of Saskatoon man who fatally stabbed spouse key in judge's 'difficult' verdict. CTV News. L. Woodward. April 7, 2021. https://saskatoon.ctvnews.ca/mental-state-of-saskatoon-man-who-fatally-stabbed-spouse-key-in-judge-s-difficult-verdict-1.5378554.
4) MRU prof victim 'very disappointed' after Supreme Court upholds extreme intoxication defence. CTV News. S. Thomas, May 13, 2022. https://calgary.ctvnews.ca/mru-prof-victim-very-disappointed-after-supreme-court-upholds-extreme-intoxication-defence-1.5902478
5) British Columbia trials drug decriminalization. National Library of Medicine. D. Duong. February 21, 2023. https://www.ncbi.nlm.nih.gov/pmc/articles/PMC9943569
6) Supreme Court of Canada Brief. R. v. Ndhlovu. October 28, 2022. https://www.scc-csc.ca/case-dossier/cb/2022/39360-eng.pdf
7) Former teacher gets non-jail sentence for child porn conviction. CBC News. April 17, 2008. https://www.cbc.ca/news/canada/saskatchewan/former-teacher-gets-non-jail-sentence-for-child-porn-conviction-1.745254
8) Statutory Release and the Parole Board of Canada - Fact Sheet. Government of Canada. https://www.canada.ca/en/parole-board/

corporate/publications-and-forms/statutory-release-and-the-parole-board-of-canada-fact-sheet.html
9) Supreme Court of Canada Unanimously Strikes Down Life Without Parole Sentences. FD.org website. https://www.fd.org/news/supreme-court-canada-unanimously-strikes-down-life-without-parole-sentences
10) Legislative Background: An Act to amend the Criminal Code, the Youth Criminal Justice Act and other Acts and to make consequential amendments to other Acts, as enacted (Bill C-75 in the 42nd Parliament). Government of Canada. https://www.justice.gc.ca/eng/rp-pr/csj-sjc/jsp-sjp/c75/p3.html
11) Ontario officer shot dead near Hagersville, Ont. was 'ambushed': OPP commissioner. S. Hassan. Canadian Press. December 28, 2022. https://globalnews.ca/news/9375256/opp-charges-fatal-shooting-officer-hagersville/

Chapter 18

1) The December 1, 1991 Referendum/Presidential Election in Ukraine. https://www.csce.gov/sites/helsinkicommission.house.gov/files/120191UkraineReferendum.pdf
2) Democracy in Ukraine: Are We There Yet? M. Minakov and M. Rojansky. October 25, 2015. https://www.wilsoncenter.org/sites/default/files/media/documents/publication/kennan_cable_30_-_rojansky_minakov.pdf
3) Jolly japes at summit show extent to which G7 leaders are out of touch with reality: China Daily editorial. China Daily. June 28, 2022 https://global.chinadaily.com.cn/a/202206/28/WS62bae6b7a310fd2b29e6918d.html
4) LNG. Newfoundland Labrador. http://www.lng-nl.com/the-project
5) Trudeau defends decision to return turbines to Germany for Russian pipeline. CBC News. D. Major. July 13, 2022. https://www.cbc.ca/news/politics/trudeau-defends-turbine-decision-russia-germany-1.6519254

Chapter 27

1) An activist in office: Steven Guilbeault's first year as environment minister. CBC News. Januaey 3, 2023. https://www.cbc.ca/news/canada/newfoundland-labrador/steven-guilbeault-environment-minister-first-year-1.6702146
2) Alberta's top court dismisses conviction appeals of wealthy Calgary businessman and a retired cop. Calgary Herald News. August 25, 2022. https://calgaryherald.com/news/crime/albertas-top-court-dismisses-conviction-appeals-of-wealthy-calgary-businessman-and-a-retired-cop
3) Justin Trudeau's 'Bollywood' wardrobe amuses Indians. BBC News. February 2018. https://www.bbc.com/news/world-asia-india-43151115
4) Convicted attempted murderer invited to reception with Trudeau in India. CBC News. T. Milewski. https://www.cbc.ca/news/politics/jaspal-atwal-invite-dinner-sophie-1.4545881
5) Do I have to justify how hard I was hit in the breast?' MP criticized after being elbowed by Trudeau. May 20, 2016. National Post. https://nationalpost.com/news/politics/do-i-have-justify-how-hard-i-was-hit-in-the-breast-mp-criticized-after-being-elbowed-by-trudeau
6) Longevity and the New Journey of Retirement. Edward Jones. 2022. https://www.edwardjones.ca/sites/default/files/acquiadam/2022-07/Edward-Jones-Age-Wave-Final-Report_CA.pdf

ABOUT THE AUTHOR

Jerry Cherneski holds a master's degree in Educational Leadership.

Raised in a small town in Saskatchewan, he spent his professional years in Moose Jaw, Saskatchewan, where he resides still today. Jerry was not only a teacher for more than 30 years, he was also a long-time coach in the sports of football, hockey and curling.

Manufactured by Amazon.ca
Bolton, ON